First published in the UK in 2005 by Circle Books
Circle Books
83/84 George Street
Richmond
Surrey TW9 1HE
Phone: 020 8332 2709

© British Sub-Aqua Club
Telford's Quay, South Pier Road
Ellesmere Port
Cheshire CH65 4FL
Phone: 0151 350 6200

Author
Kris Pedder

Editor
Charles Hood

Design
Ian Legge

Illustrations: Ian Legge
Photographs: Charles Hood

Print
Printed in China for Compass Press Limited
162–164 Upper Richmond Road
London SW15 2SL
Phone: 020 8780 7000

ISBN: 0-9538919-7-6

Seamanship:
a guide for divers

Foreword

As National Diving Officer of the world's largest dive club I am extremely proud to have been asked to present this new edition of the BSAC's manual *Seamanship: a guide for divers*.

Divers naturally crave to diversify and deepen their knowledge of all aspects of their sport and the British Sub-Aqua Club exists to support its members in the attainment of new understanding through varied and inspiring Skill Development Courses. The result is a club of divers who are not only skilled in conducting diving operations, but are also competent, 'rounded' divers with expertise in a number of diving-related activities. Often these divers have come to understand the thrill of successfully, independently and safely navigating a boat to new dive sites and, through knowledge of tides, charts and electronic aids, are able to predict the underwater conditions for a dive.

No text can replace the experience of going to sea with competent, experienced instructors who can guide you through the practical lessons to be learned about seamanship. However, this volume does prepare divers for their first experiences of going to sea to dive and it also serves as a reference manual for divers wishing to improve on many aspects of diving-related seamanship.

Over the years I have had the good fortune to dive with some of the BSAC's great adventurers and through them have experienced dives in the remotest parts of the UK and the excitement of independent exploration. This manual represents the beginning of an expedition of understanding, fun and adventure.

Clare Peddie
National Diving Officer
British Sub-Aqua Club

Table of contents

Contents **9**

Introduction

As divers, we want to be underwater as much as we can. However, we need to get to the dive site and this often involves a boat journey. This book is designed to give the aspiring diver coxswain a grounding in all the skills they are likely to need.

Being the skipper of a diving boat is great fun. For most of the time it is safe and enjoyable. However, there are essential things to understand and practice in order to prevent accidents. Travelling at high speed, in confined waters, on a collision course with another vessel, is hardly the best time to wonder whether the correct thing to do is to turn to port or starboard. We start by introducing some nautical terms and move straight on to how to actually drive a small dive boat. Day-to-day skills, such as turning in a confined space, are clearly talked through and illustrated.

There is a detailed section on working with ropes. Basic maintenance of outboard engines is crucial, especially when neglect can mean the difference between a dive or a day spent grumbling in a boatyard. And you have a duty to understand the law as it applies to boats and trailers. There are, of course, rules and regulations applying to vessels at sea too.

Things can go wrong, emergencies happen. But to prevent a minor mishap turning into a life-threatening incident you need to apply some basic safety procedures. We take you through the most common emergency situations and how to address them.

As coxswain, you are responsible for your divers and crew, and voyage planning has become an important feature of the job. So you will need to learn how to find your way at sea and how to assess the weather. Using transits, GPS and echo sounders makes it relatively easy to find a dive site. Lastly, some divers prefer to let others take the helm. What should you look out for when chartering a diving vessel and how can you assist the skipper to make sure your day is enjoyable and incident free?

By the end of this book, and with some skill development courses under your belt, we hope you will have gained valuable insights into the world of diving and small boats. Enjoy.

Nautical terms

In order to talk about boats we need to use various technical terms, known to all seafarers. It seems sensible to introduce them at the beginning of this book and to use them throughout. These terms give us a precise way of describing boats and what is happening on board. The most useful ones are given here.

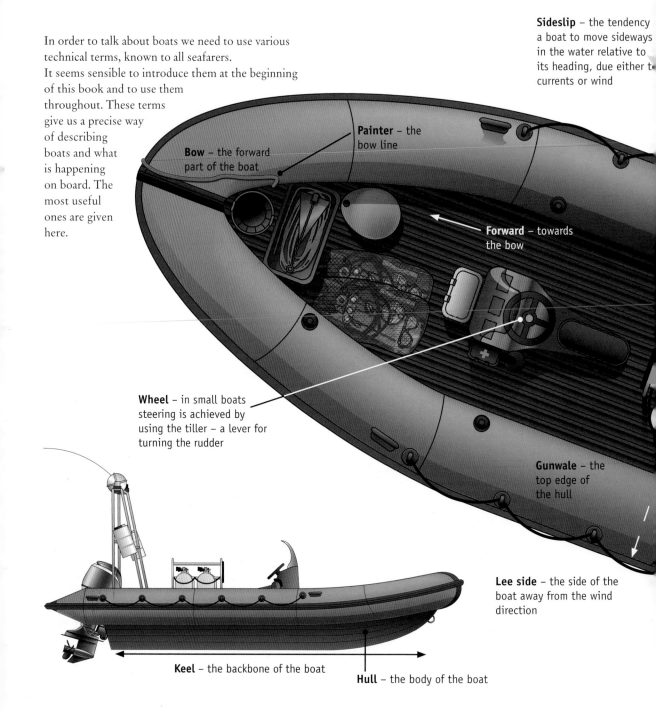

Sideslip – the tendency a boat to move sideways in the water relative to its heading, due either t currents or wind

Painter – the bow line

Bow – the forward part of the boat

Forward – towards the bow

Wheel – in small boats steering is achieved by using the tiller – a lever for turning the rudder

Gunwale – the top edge of the hull

Lee side – the side of the boat away from the wind direction

Keel – the backbone of the boat

Hull – the body of the boat

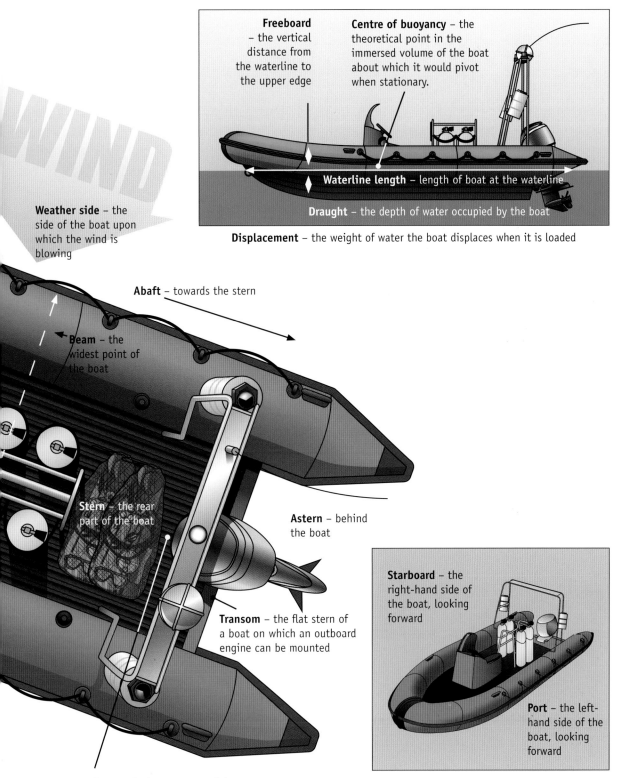

Freeboard – the vertical distance from the waterline to the upper edge

Centre of buoyancy – the theoretical point in the immersed volume of the boat about which it would pivot when stationary.

Waterline length – length of boat at the waterline

Draught – the depth of water occupied by the boat

Displacement – the weight of water the boat displaces when it is loaded

Weather side – the side of the boat upon which the wind is blowing

Abaft – towards the stern

Beam – the widest point of the boat

Stern – the rear part of the boat

Astern – behind the boat

Transom – the flat stern of a boat on which an outboard engine can be mounted

Starboard – the right-hand side of the boat, looking forward

Port – the left-hand side of the boat, looking forward

Bilges – the bottom part of the boat where any water collects

Nautical terms **13**

Chapter one

Using small boats

Most of the time a dive boat is a workboat, transporting divers and their kit as quickly, comfortably and safely as possible to the dive site. It also has to act as a stable platform from which to conduct the diving operations. If you are doing it yourself, then you also want the boat to be easy to move by road and simple to launch and recover. A very small boat can easily be carried over the beach to launch, but may not have space for all of your equipment.

Divers find themselves at sea in varying weather and sea conditions and the dive boat must be able to cope with this. Buoyancy is key here: essentially, we need enough to support the boat, its engine and fittings, and the divers and their equipment. From a diving point of view, the bigger the deck space the better, as it will be easier to get organised and kit-up. Stability during kitting-up helps, as does an easy way of getting in and out of the water.

The speed of your boat and the comfort of its passengers are affected by the sea state, the hull type, the propulsion system and the load. And, of course, the fuel consumption, due to any combination of these, will have an effect on your finances.

No wonder there is always some compromise when choosing a dive boat. In general, dive boats are between 3 and 8 metres in length and are powered by 30 to 200 horsepower (hp) engines – two-stroke, four-stroke or diesel, outboard or inboard.

Legislation

Legislation governing boats used for leisure

In the UK, vessels less than 13.7 metres in length and used for pleasure only are classed as non-regulated pleasure vessels (NRPVs) and they are unregulated as far as lifesaving or fire-fighting equipment is concerned. The UK Safety Afloat scheme, a voluntary code of best and safe practice for leisure craft users, makes recommendations for this class of vessel. Copies of *Safety Afloat* are available from the Maritime and Coastguard Agency (MCA). NRPVs more than 13.7 metres long are defined as class XII vessels and must comply with the appropriate Merchant Shipping Regulations for life-saving and fire-protection equipment. Most club dive boats in the UK are less than 13.7 metres.

Included in the definition of pleasure vessels used in the current legislation are those vessels wholly owned by a members' club. To properly claim to be such a vessel the boat must be in the ownership of the club as a legal entity, or in the joint ownership of all the members evidenced by documentation that is legally binding on all parties. And the major and valuable items of equipment for the vessel must be similarly owned and evidenced. The members' club must be able to produce its own constitution, membership list and accounts to an officer of the MCA, when required to produce ship's documents under the provisions of section 257 of The Merchant Shipping Act 1995.

A members' club means an affiliated club under the rules of which a member may not be admitted to membership, or as a candidate for membership, without an interval of at least two days between nomination or application and admission. Any profits of the club may not be distributed to the members of the club.

It is considered acceptable to invite guests on diving trips on boats operated by members' clubs providing that the following criteria are met:

- Any costs to the guest will be limited to actual running costs for that trip only
- No additional charge or levy be made
- A temporary membership fee is not an acceptable means of imposing a levy
- The number of visits as a guest should be restricted to six in any calendar year.

The government has also set out objectives for sport, but the principle of self-determination for sports bodies has been encouraged to the extent that when it has been necessary to impose some form of control on such bodies, the policy has usually been to encourage the bodies to adopt voluntary codes or procedures that would have the same effect as regulation. The British Sub-Aqua Club (BSAC), The Professional Association of Diving Instructors (PADI), The Scottish Sub-Aqua Club (SSAC) and The Sub-Aqua Association (SAA) have worked together in the UK as the Combined Diving Associations (CDA) to issue guidance on the safe practice of the sport of scuba diving. The CDA document *Guidelines for the Safe Operation of Member Club Dive Boats* was the result of a forum discussion with the MCA and the Royal National Lifeboat Insititution (RNLI). It contains safety information for those involved in club diving. Further details are available on CDA member association websites (see *Useful organisations*, page 176).

Types of small boats

Inflatable boats

Inflatable boats consist of at least two air-filled side tubes, meeting at the bow, a flexible hull with either a rigid or inflatable keel, and a solid floor and solid transom. An outboard engine can be mounted on the transom, usually with a separate fuel tank and tiller steering.

These boats are completely collapsible, but because of this their hull is rather flexible. This adversely affects handling, and inflatables suffer from a tendency to skid in high-speed turns and are not very responsive at slow speeds. They are, however, designed to plane – that is, to ride on top of the water at relatively high speeds – and this makes them fast and economical on fuel.

RIBs are highly manoeuvrable, making them both fun and extremely practical for divers

The overall rigidity of the boat comes from the air pressure in the tubes. In the heat of the sun, damage can be caused by the increasing tube pressure, which should be released as soon as possible. On the other hand, putting the boat into the water, and cooling the tubes, can reduce the tube pressure and make the boat too soft - which affects the handling. In extreme cases this could cause the floorboards to move and the boat to collapse.

There is little opportunity to successfully mount navigational equipment in an inflatable boat. A power supply is difficult to arrange and the bouncy, wet ride can cause havoc with the electronics.

Having said all this, it is difficult to sink an inflatable boat. They have the attraction of being truly portable, buoyant and stable. But they do suffer from lack of space on board and make for an uncomfortable ride in any significant sea. Once the most popular type of dive boat in the UK, inflatables have largely been supplanted by the rigid-hulled inflatable boat.

Rigid-hulled inflatables

These have a rigid hull, usually made of glass fibre reinforced plastic (GRP) surmounted by air-filled tubes. RIBs can be powered by either inboard or outboard engines. These can be two-strokes, four-strokes or diesels.

At rest, the RIB is supported by the buoyancy of its tubes. When moving, the tubes rise above the water as the boat planes on its rigid hull. RIBs usually have forward controls at a centre console, which may also house an integral fuel tank and a battery. Thus they can easily support electronic equipment and an electric start system for the engine.

They are generally either kept moored or transported by trailer. Ancillary equipment can be conveniently stored in the boat at all times, but you must be aware that there are legal limits on the allowable weight of the trailer (see *Trailers and the UK law*, page 76).

RIBs are highly manoeuvrable and almost unsinkable. At high speed, they handle extremely well and provide a more comfortable ride than inflatables. At low speeds they act as displacement hulls, with corresponding good handling.

Storage space on board RIBs is often increased by the use of a cylinder rack, fixed to the solid floor, to store diving cylinders vertically. It is also possible to have a forward locker of some sort. The addition of an A-frame at the stern provides a place to attach navigation lights, storage boxes containing flares, the first aid-kit and tools.

Types of small boats

Inboard diesel engines are more efficient than outboards

Twin outboards offer safety but add to the cost and weight of the boat

Types of small boats

Solid-hulled boats

Small solid-hulled boats are also of interest to divers. Such boats have large deck spaces because of their steep sides and blunt bows, and being broad across the beam, they are relatively stable at rest. The hull can take a variety of forms, and all are designed to plane for comfort and economy. They will have some buoyancy built in, but usually not enough to support a flooded boat. Such boats are again kept moored or launched from a trailer. They may provide more shelter from the elements, in the form of a forward cabin, which gives a drier ride.

A small inflatable dive boat with tiller steering

Loading

Loading the boat

A RIB travelling at slow speed will act as if it were a displacement hull: one that is driven through the water. The three forces acting on the boat are the engine's propulsive force, the force of the water it is travelling through and the effect of the wind. If the water or the wind is moving in the same direction as the boat, its speed will be added to that of the boat, increasing the boat's speed over the ground. If the water or the wind is moving in the opposite direction to the boat, it will reduce the effective speed of the boat. When the water or the wind is moving across the boat's line of travel, the boat will be pushed sideways.

Once you are travelling on the plane at high speed, the effect of the boat's water displacement is minimised, but the effect of the wind still needs to be considered. Strong sideways gusts can be quite noticeable. When travelling into the wind and cresting a wave, the wind can exert a strong lifting force on the hull. A similar effect is seen when performing high-speed turns in these conditions. It is possible that these manoeuvres could lead to capsize (see *Capsized boat*, page 109).

The boat's load – both people and equipment – will also affect how the boat handles. Loading the boat is the coxswain's responsibility. It is best to keep the equipment load evenly distributed, in a way that maintains the boat's centre of gravity. Cylinders need to be prevented from moving during a journey, to avoid damage to the boat, the divers and crew, and the cylinders. Basic kit is best stored in bags to prevent loss or damage. In order to make it easy for the divers to kit up when you are on site, it makes sense to keep a buddy pair's diving equipment together.

The most comfortable ride in a RIB or inflatable is towards the rear, as the bow tends to bounce up and down more than the stern. It may be necessary, depending on the weight of the crew, for the coxswain to move people forward to help the boat onto the plane. Once on the plane they can return to a more comfortable position.

In an unladen boat, you need enough weight in the form of crew to hold the bows down. The manufacturer's specification for a RIB or inflatable should be clearly displayed on a plate mounted inside the boat. This will include details of the maximum load that the boat is designed to carry and the maximum engine size it will support.

At slow speeds the hull is pushed through the water

On the plane there is minimal contact between hull and water

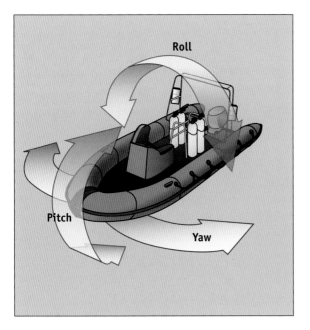

Motion at sea

In any kind of sea, a vessel is subject to three types of rotational movement: roll, pitch and yaw.

Roll is a side-to-side rotation about the boat's fore-to-aft (or longitudinal) axis, usually near the waterline. A boat that rolls fast, often and deeply gives an uncomfortable ride.

Pitch is the up and down motion of the bow and stern around the boat's beam-to-beam (lateral) axis.

Yaw is a back-and-forth weaving motion in the boat's course in response to being pushed about by waves. The axis of the movement is vertical. The rudder initiates a yawing movement to turn the boat. Boats with high directional stability tend to yaw less in response to the waves.

The result of movement about all these axes is that amidships, or slightly aft, is the part of the boat that moves the least in all three directions. This affects the comfort of the ride and on larger boats the comfort of the accommodation. Bunks at the bow of the boat are uncomfortable in heavier seas.

The Recreational Craft Directive (RCD)

All recreational craft between 2.5 and 24 metres hull length built in or imported into the European Union, are assessed under the RCD. Once a satisfactory assessment is completed, the following information is displayed on each individual boat made, in the form of a builder's specification plate.

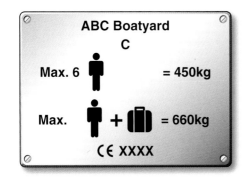

Design categories

A) Ocean – a largely self-sufficient vessel able to undertake extended voyages in force 8 winds and waves more than 4 metres

B) Offshore – offshore voyages in force 8 winds and waves up to 4 metres

C) Inshore – voyages in coastal waters, estuaries, lakes and rivers in force 6 winds and waves of 2 metres

D) Sheltered waters – voyages on small lakes, rivers and canals in force 4 winds and waves of 0.5 metres

Maximum number of persons - of average weight 75 kilograms

Maximum recommended load - including people, baggage, equipment and fuel, but excluding fuel and water in fixed tanks

CE mark - indicates that the boat complies with the Recreational Craft Directive. Boats of less than 12 metres may show a notified body's identification number instead.

Also, every craft will have a hull identification number. This is separate from the builder's plate and is marked on the transom and on another hidden location.

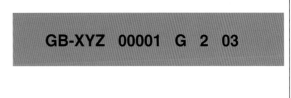

Essential equipment

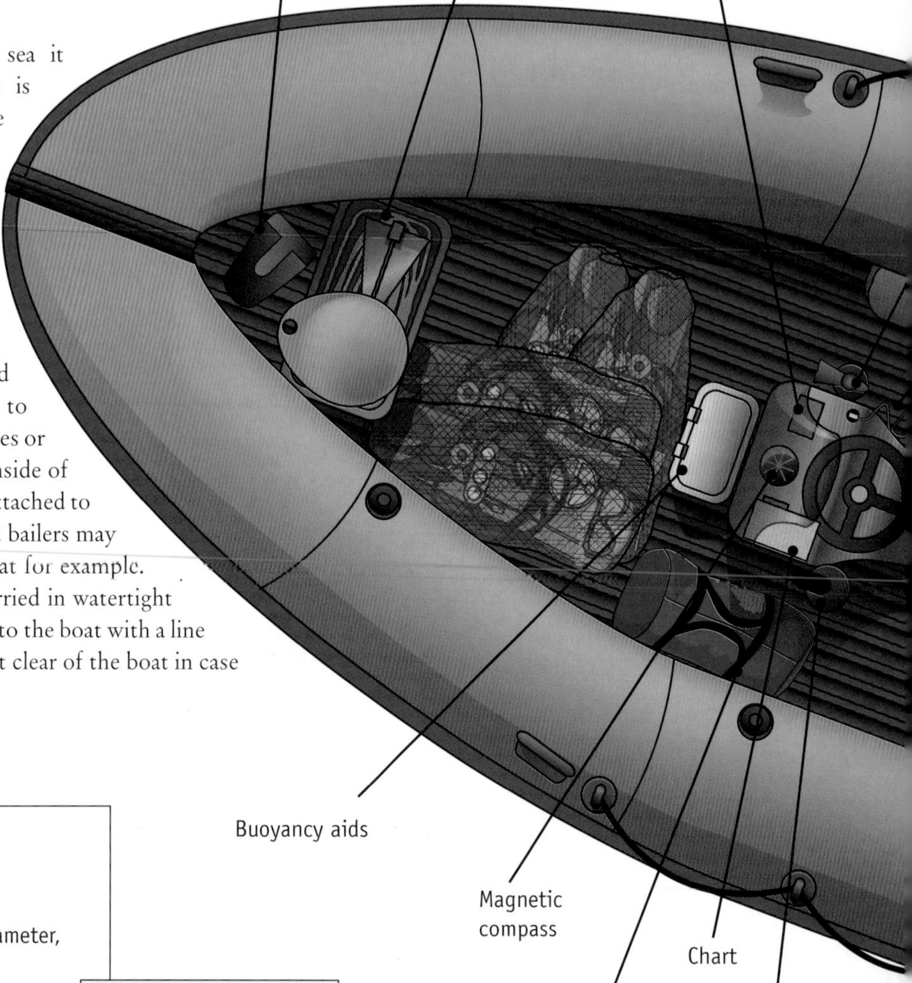

Before taking a boat out to sea it is important to check that it is kitted out with the appropriate equipment, and that this is all in good working order. This is the responsibility of the coxswain. The labelled diagram shows equipment that is essential in a small boat.

Because small dive boats generally offer little enclosed storage space, items often need to be attached to something. Paddles or oars can be secured along the inside of the tubes. Fuel cans should be attached to the boat with a line. Pumps and bailers may fit into a locker, beneath the seat for example. Safety equipment should be carried in watertight emergency boxes. Attach these to the boat with a line long enough for the box to float clear of the boat in case of capsize.

Bailer

Anchor, rope, chain and buoy

Navigation instruments
VHF radio
Clock/watch

Buoyancy aids

Magnetic compass

Chart

Personal protective clothing

Fire extinguisher(s)

Recommended equipment
Oxygen administration kit
Knife
Mooring lines 10-12 mm in diameter, 10 metres long
Handheld VHF radio
GMDSS/DSC radio
EPIRB (see page 104)
Reserve fuel
Echo sounder
Electronic navigational aids (GPS)
Searchlight
Hand compass
Throwing line/throwing bag and float

Ancillary Equipment
Shot-lines
Towing bridle
Sea anchor
Diver recall signals

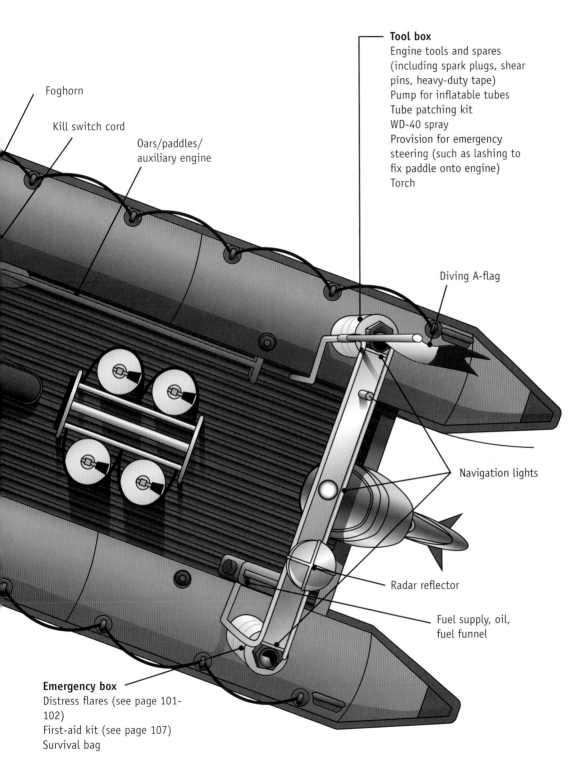

Foghorn

Kill switch cord

Oars/paddles/
auxiliary engine

Tool box
Engine tools and spares
(including spark plugs, shear
pins, heavy-duty tape)
Pump for inflatable tubes
Tube patching kit
WD-40 spray
Provision for emergency
steering (such as lashing to
fix paddle onto engine)
Torch

Diving A-flag

Navigation lights

Radar reflector

Fuel supply, oil,
fuel funnel

Emergency box
Distress flares (see page 101-
102)
First-aid kit (see page 107)
Survival bag

Using small boats **23**

Preparing the boat

Launching

Launch site

To launch a boat such as a RIB or dory from a trailer, you need to find suitable access to the sea. This could be a firm beach, but is more likely to be a slipway. You will need to check that the slipway has access to the water at your proposed launch time. Descriptions of slipways in books or on internet sites usually give you an idea of how many hours each side of high water you can use the slipway. Not all slipways are useable in all weathers: wind direction and strength will affect the water conditions on the slip. Even small-looking waves can make it awkward, if not dangerous, to launch.

All slipways belong to someone – this might be a harbour authority, a local authority, a business, or a private individual. There is often a daily launching fee to pay and there will be rules to be observed, including where to leave trailers. A telephone call to the owner will mean you have up-to-date information to help with your launch, and all parties will be happy.

Preparing the boat

It makes sense to prepare the boat before driving onto the slipway and the less time you spend hogging the slip, the more time there is available for others to launch. You will need to remove all towing gear, such as any boat cover, propeller cover, light board, and fixing straps. Navigational aids, radio, aerials and other boat equipment can then be assembled and fitted.

Before launching, the coxswain should check the boat, engine and ancillary equipment. It is far easier to rectify any problems ashore than on the water.

- Check for obvious problems with the hull and tubes.
- Check the power supply to the radio, navigational lights and other electronic aids.
- Look over the engine for obvious faults and check the correct functioning of the controls.
- Ensure that the fuel supply is adequate for your journey. The UK's 'Safety Afloat' scheme

recommends that you have one third of your fuel in reserve on any journey. Remember to add oil for 2 strokes or top up oil for 4 strokes as necessary. If you are planning to use spare cans of fuel, make sure that they contain the correct mixture of fuel and oil.

- Check that the boat's working and safety equipment and diving first aid equipment are present and correctly stowed.
- Check with the dive marshal that the dive log sheets are stowed along with any information needed to locate the dive site, such as details of transits.

Launching from a trailer

Now you are ready to drive onto the slipway. At this stage it is useful to have some divers dressed in their suits ready to help. All those involved in the launch should understand that, to avoid accidents, they must not stand behind the trailer. They should also keep well clear whenever the trailer is being manoeuvred.

In most cases you will have to reverse down to the water. However, if there is enough hard standing or firm beach at the base of the slipway, you could drive down and turn at the bottom. Someone should be nominated to take charge of the boat when it leaves the trailer, even if that only means holding the painter. On other occasions it may be possible to launch the boat with a coxswain on board.

Back the trailer down to the water's edge. Make sure that the engine is tilted upwards. Remember to undo the winch strap at the bow. The only thing keeping the boat on the trailer at this stage should be gravity. It may not be necessary to submerge the trailer in order to launch. In fact it is probably better to keep the hubs dry, as salt water will damage the wheel bearings (see *Boat Trailers*, page 75). When there is enough water under the boat to prevent grounding, one person on either side of the nose should be able to start the boat moving off the trailer. Take care that the painter does not get caught up in the

Check that all straps have been removed

Back the trailer to the water's edge

Push the boat off the trailer

Move away from the trailer

trailer as the boat moves off. Once the boat is clear of the trailer you can vacate the slipway for the next user.

If conditions at the bottom of the slipway make you reluctant to drive your vehicle any further, it is possible to unhook the trailer and manhandle it to the water's edge. While the trailer tyres will manage quite well on sand, the jockey wheel may not: it tends to dig into the sand. One solution is to release the weight on the nose of the boat by

moving the load, but better still you can install a sand tyre on your trailer (see photograph overleaf). This system stows the spare wheel at the front of the trailer in such a way that it can be lowered to act as a third rolling wheel when needed.

Launching an inflatable

The sand tyre allows the trailer to move on the beach

Safety briefing

Launching an inflatable

An inflatable boat can be launched from a trailer in the same way as a RIB, although it is likely that the trailer will have to be submerged further. Inflatable trailers tend not to use rollers and so the boat has to be floated on and off the trailer.

If an exciting dive site beckons from an inhospitable shore, an inflatable could be carried to the water's edge. The largest piece of equipment to be carried down is the boat, without its engine. This will probably require the whole dive team. Depending on sea conditions, you may be able to put the boat straight into the water. The outboard engine will need two people to carry it. If conditions permit, it should be put directly onto the transom, bolted on and secured with a strop. In a swell, tilt the engine to avoid damaging the propeller. The rest of the boat's equipment can be assembled at the water's edge and loaded by the coxswain.

If there are breaking waves you will need to keep the bow into the waves and this will probably take at least two people. As soon as possible, move the boat beyond the breaking waves and wait there: your divers will find it easier to wade out to the boat.

Getting underway

Before loading any divers, it is the coxswain's responsibility to check that the engine starts and runs, that the tubes are fully inflated and that the ancillary equipment is present and stowed correctly. You will also need to give the divers and crew a safety briefing, which is used to explain the safety aspects of the boat and the equipment carried onboard.

The coxswain should cover each of the following, indicating its location and any other essential information.

• Lifejackets
• VHF radio and emergency use
• First aid kit
• Oxygen kit
• Flares
• Tool kit and spares
• Fire extinguisher(s)
• Kill switch cord
• Fuel isolation valve
• Any additional safety equipment specific to the craft
• Stowage of diving equipment for safe operation
• Planned route and times
• Expected conditions

Starting the engine

- Ensure sufficient depth between the propeller and the sea bed. Engines may be started on tilt as long as the cooling water inlets are submerged. They may be noisy if the exhaust ports remain uncovered.

- Connect the fuel line to the engine, open the fuel tank vent, and then prime the in-line rubber bulb until hard. Check you have sufficient fuel. The UK coastguard's *Safety Afloat* recommends that you keep a third of your total fuel in reserve. Remember that fuel consumption will increase in rougher seas and if you are travelling against the wind and tide.

- Check that the gear lever is in the neutral position.

- If a kill switch is fitted, check that it is connected correctly.

- Modern engines have an automatic choke. For engines with a manual choke, only experience will tell you how much choke to use. Generally you will need the choke to start a cold engine. You may not need it to start a warm engine. Too much choke may cause the engine to flood and it will not start. The simple solution is to leave it for 10 minutes for the excess fuel to evaporate.

- Having made sure that no one is standing around the propeller, start the engine. If you have electric start, do not try for longer than 20 seconds. If your engine is fitted with a pull-cord, hold the toggle and take up the slack, then firmly pull the cord. Let the cord re-coil itself automatically. You may need to adjust the fast idle and/or the manual choke, and try again.

- When the engine fires, check the 'telltale' jet to see whether cooling water is coming out. If not stop the engine and check the inlet ports. If at any stage the water in the telltale jet becomes hot it is a sign that something is wrong and you should stop the engine immediately.

- After running the engine for a minute or two, reduce the fast idle or push in the manual choke. The engine should idle evenly.

- When going forwards in shallow water it is advisable to run the engine on tilt. For an engine with a manual tilt lock, disengage the tilt lock so that the engine can swing up if it hits an obstacle. Engines with a manual tilt-lock should have this engaged before they are put into reverse gear, otherwise the engine will swing upwards.

- Before you put the engine into gear you must always let the engine speed drop to tick-over. Always be positive about changing gear. Do not hesitate, as tentative action tends to damage the gears.

- Motor around for a few minutes before setting off on your journey. Make sure that you are not alone in the boat and that the ancillary equipment has been loaded first.

Turning

Boat handling skills

Boat handling is a skill that should be learned on a boat-handling course and then practised. Any kind of manoeuvre in a boat requires you to think ahead and plan the move. You must bear in mind the water conditions at the time. Unlike a car, a boat only has two controls, a throttle and a gear lever – no brakes. Braking is achieved either by easing off the throttle, using the wind and the current, or using reverse gear. Look out for water coming in at the stern when you reverse. Moving at slow speed will minimise this. Remember, in reverse gear the direction that you steer in will be reversed. Engines with a manual tilt lock should have this engaged before selecting reverse gear otherwise the engine will lift up out of the water as you open the throttle.

The crew and divers travelling in a small boat should always hold on to the boat when it is underway.

Stopping and starting

Right from the start you must acquaint yourself with the sensitivity of the steering and the throttle. You must gain confidence with this before attempting any other manoeuvres. The throttle should be opened up gradually to gain speed and move onto the plane. The boat will lose way quickly when the throttle is closed, that is you will lose any steering – but you will drift for some distance, so you must slow down in plenty of time.

Turning

To turn the boat, if you have a wheel you turn the wheel in the direction that you wish to go. If you have tiller steering, place the tiller in the direction away from your intended turn. At slow speeds it will seem as if the boat takes a long time to respond. You will have to think ahead.

What you are doing is directing the thrust of the propeller so that the bow of the boat is turned towards the desired direction. When a boat turns the stern moves out and the pivoting point is close to the bow – rather like

rear wheel steering on land. Turns can be speeded up or tightened by increasing the power but care should be taken and clear warning given as this could lead to a person falling overboard or a swamped boat.

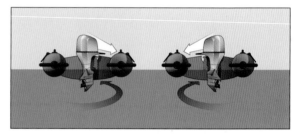

Turning to port and starboard using a tiller

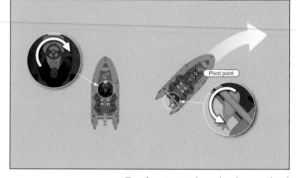

Turning to starboard using a wheel

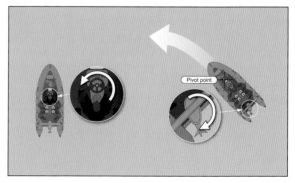

Turning to port using a wheel

A straight-line approach at slow speed gives the best result

Picking up a mooring

This is not difficult if you remember to use the wind or tide – whichever is having the biggest braking effect on the boat. Give yourself as much sea room as possible. Approach the mooring buoy in a straight line and reduce speed as you come closer, until you have almost stopped. As you reach the buoy put the engine into neutral. Approach slowly, because it is always easier to increase speed suddenly rather than to decrease it. Having decided in advance which side of the boat you want to take the mooring, you reach out and grab it. Have a line prepared to use to tie up to the mooring buoy.

Coming alongside

Coming alongside

In this circumstance you are putting your boat against a large, hard jetty or quay that may well have its own local eddies and wave reflections for you to contend with. Wind and tide can still be used to help.

If you are approaching a berth into wind, approach at an angle of 30 degrees or against the tidal stream. With practice you will be able to hold the bow against the berth, using the engine, until it is secure, before using a stern line to pull in the stern of the boat.

For a downwind landing you must get the positioning of your approach just right, as your speed is out of your control. You may have to use reverse gear to control the boat on approach, but remember the steering will be reversed. The throttle must be used gently in this situation.

Leaving a quay

An offshore wind will make leaving a berth easy – if nothing else, you will get blown offshore. But with an onshore wind it will be more difficult. A successful method is to leave in reverse, stern first, allowing the boat to pivot around the bow to avoid scraping along the quay, and giving yourself plenty of room before turning to head into wind.

Another way of leaving a berth in an onshore wind is to release the stern line, steer as if to drive into the berth, and go ahead slowly. The stern will move out. When you are nearly at right angles to the berth, steer the other way, let go of the bow line and go into reverse. This will bring you clear of the berth and roughly parallel to it, then you can move off.

Coming alongside against an offshore wind

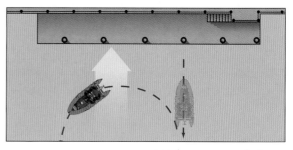

Leaving a quay against an onshore wind

Handling at speed

Boats such as RIBs, inflatables and dories are capable of travelling efficiently at high speeds by planing. To move a boat onto the plane, open the throttle firmly. As the boat picks up speed the bow will rise as a wall of water builds up under the bows. This is when the hull begins its transition from acting like a displacement hull to acting like a planing hull.

As the boat climbs over the 'hump', the bow will begin to settle to a level position, with only the deepest parts of the hull in the water. You can throttle back without loss of speed as the boat is now planing. Powering back will reduce fuel consumption without affecting your speed. With a lightly loaded boat you should be careful when getting onto the plane, as a headwind could increase the already high angle of the bows enough to flip the boat over.

A boat must have enough power to get onto the plane. If it is on the limits, redistributing the load or changing the tilt of the engine may help.

Always decrease your speed slowly. If you slow down suddenly, the boat will come off the plane in a short distance and the following wave will catch the boat and break over the stern. Also, by making sudden changes in speed you additionally run the risk of throwing a person overboard.

Turning in a confined area

Making a three-point turn in a confined space is a difficult manoeuvre. Let's start our turn to port: steer hard to port giving a short burst of throttle, throttle back and go into neutral. As the stern begins to swing, steer hard to starboard, engage reverse and give the throttle a short burst. As the boat begins to turn towards your exit, go into neutral. Then drive out of the confined area. Remember that if your engine has a manual tilt lock, it must be on lock when you use reverse.

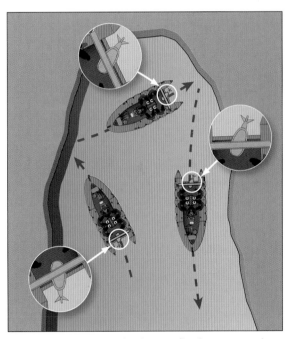

When turning in a confined area, remember the engine will move the stern of the boat and the bow will be the pivoting point

Handling in rough weather

Handling in rough weather

Even small waves can mean a rough, bouncy ride in a small boat. The ride depends in part on the length of your boat and the distance between the waves. If you are travelling head-on to the waves and the distance between them is short enough to be uncomfortable, you can alter course to follow a zigzag pattern and make turns across the waves by up to 45 degrees – this will lengthen the apparent distance between waves and increase the comfort for your divers and crew.

As the wind approaches 4 to 5 on the Beaufort wind scale, you should be wondering whether or not to launch your small boat. But conditions at sea can change rapidly and you may unexpectedly have to deal with rough weather while you are out. Opposing wind and tide, or changes in tidal flow, can also cause isolated patches of rough water. As the waves increase, your speed will have to decrease, or you risk damage to both your boat and the people in it. In rough water, instruct your divers and crew to make sure they maintain a good hold on the boat.

When heading into the waves, keep the boat bows into the waves. Turning broadside on – known as broaching – in breaking waves could easily lead to swamping or the boat capsizing. Apply enough power to climb the waves and be ready to decrease the power at the crest of the wave to avoid taking to the air and crashing down into the next trough. As well as that being uncomfortable for the passengers, you could damage the boat.

If your course takes you across large waves, it may be easier to run along the troughs, waiting for a good moment to cross the next wave. In this way you might make better progress and use less fuel, even though you cover a greater distance.

Running with a following sea, when the waves come from astern, is much more difficult and can be dangerous if care is not taken. You will have less control over the boat as you are pushed along by the waves. You will need to control the boat rather than allowing the sea to control it, so you will need to continually adjust your speed,

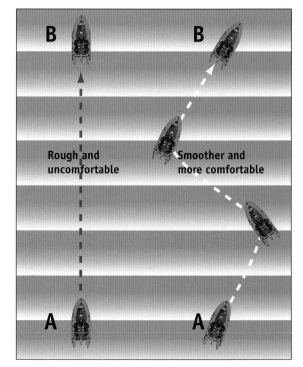

Taking a diagonal path across the waves improves the ride for the passengers

keeping a good lookout behind you. You must never try to surf the wave – that is, never travel at the same speed as a following wave. Try to move either faster than waves coming from astern, so that you overtake them, or move slower than them, so that they overtake you.

The only way to protect and control the boat as it meets a wall of water is to make the bows as high as possible. If you are planing, decreasing speed will lift the bows. If you are not on the plane, increasing speed will lift the bows.

If you are travelling faster than the waves in a following sea, you may feel that you are about to drive into the back of the wave ahead. Reduce your speed and as the boat drops off the plane the bows will lift and you can climb up the back of the wave and over the crest. Increasing your speed on the way down the front of the wave will lift the bow and get you back onto the plane.

If you are travelling more slowly than the waves in a following sea, the steep front of the next wave will lift the stern and dig the bows in. You should increase your speed to lift the bows as the wave passes and then reduce speed until the next overtaking wave reaches you.

Beaching in calm conditions

In calm conditions it is simple to approach the shore and land people and kit. As you drive towards the shore, tilt the engine or put a manual tilt lock onto tilt – this means that if the engine's skeg hits anything, the whole engine will tilt upwards, reducing any damage. Engines can be run on tilt, as long as the cooling water inlet ports are covered – you can tell if this is so by watching for the telltale water spout.

Watch out for other water users, especially swimmers and divers, who are harder to see. Prime two members of your divers or crew, sitting at the bow of the boat, to be ready to jump out and hold the boat as directed by you. No one should leave the boat without your permission, as you are in control of the engine. When you are in shallow enough water for your divers and crew to stand up, switch off the engine and put it on tilt. Coast towards the shore, and when you are ready, ask your divers and crew to jump out and hold the boat. Remember that those wearing diving suits will have some inherent buoyancy and may not be able to hold their footing in deeper water. In general, the boat should be kept out of any breaking waves.

On some occasions it may be possible to run aground. This depends on the angle of the beach, what it is made of and the state of the sea. Small boats can be hauled up onto sand or shingle beaches. On a rocky shore, you will have to take care to avoid contact with the land.

Tilt the engine as you approach the shore

When the water is shallow enough, ask your divers to jump out and hold the boat

Landing in surf

With a small boat you can follow a wave in and, in shallow water, your divers can turn the boat bow to the waves and hold its position

Landing in surf or rough water

If you have to land in rough sea conditions, you will need to study the beach carefully first. Depending on wind and tide, there may well be an area of calmer water somewhere that you should aim for. If the boat turns broadside on to the waves at any time, there is a danger of capsizing. If the boat remains stern to the waves, you may get swamped.

With a smaller boat, you can go in bow first, following a wave behind the crest, engine tilted up or with the tilt lock set to off, divers and crew ready to jump out. Once you have applied enough power to reach the shallows, turn off the engine, tilt it right up and instruct the divers and crew to jump out and either carry the boat up the shore or turn it bow into the waves.

It can be hard to hold onto a boat in such conditions and a technique called kedging can help. Position yourself several metres offshore of any breaking waves, bows to sea. Lay out your anchor and pay out the rope. Do not use your engine, but keep it running and in neutral. Keep your bows into the waves and hold up on the rope as each wave passes beneath the boat. Once you are close to shore you can land divers and equipment then retrieve your anchor and either beach the unladen boat with the help of the divers and crew on the beach or alternatively, you can moor in calmer water, the coxswain and one crew member swimming to shore. If you do this remember to keep your basic equipment with you so that you are mobile in the water.

Dropping off divers

No wind or current

1 Motor at slow speed towards the buoy, so that it is on the same side of the boat as your divers.

2 Stop beside the buoy, put the engine into neutral.

3 Give the command to enter the water.

4 When the divers are clear of the boat, and on the shot, move off in reverse and turn to keep your bow towards the divers.

Wind, no current

1 Motor at slow speed into the wind towards the buoy, so that it is on the same side of the boat as your divers.

2 Stop beside the buoy, put the engine into neutral.

3 Give the command to enter the water.

4 When the divers are on the shot, you will already have been blown away downwind.

5 When you are clear, move off in reverse.

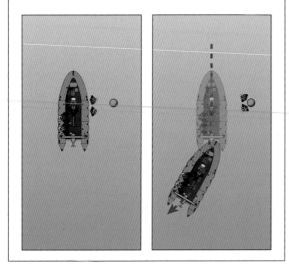

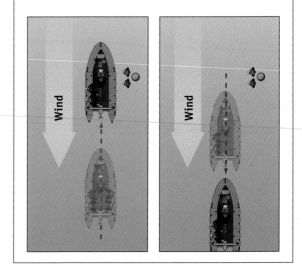

Dropping off divers

Putting divers into the water must always be done with great care. People and propellers are suddenly in close proximity and a mistake could lead to an accident. The same applies to picking up divers.

The way in which a pair of divers is dropped in at the beginning of the dive can make a great deal of difference to the dive itself. A stressful entry and a long surface swim before descending can decrease a diver's capability of resolving any subsequent problems that might arise during the dive. This is often described as being on the slopes of the incident pit, where minor problems escalate into more serious ones, causing you to slide further into trouble.

So, what makes a good start to a dive? How you choose to drop your divers may well depend upon the nature of the dive site. First, it is the coxswain's responsibility to coordinate the position fixing and the deployment of the shot line if one is being used. While this is going on and your divers are kitting up, you should be checking the effects of wind and tide on site.

The direction of the current and the wind will determine where you should drop the divers, relative to your fixed datum, whether it is a shot-line or a natural feature. Once you have decided which way the divers will drift in the water, you can decide how to approach.

Current, no wind

1 Motor at slow speed into the current. Go past the buoy, keeping it on the same side of the boat as your divers.
2 Stop when you have passed the buoy and when you judge that there is enough room, between you and the buoy, for your divers to enter the water, right themselves and find the shot while drifting towards it with the current.
3 Put the engine into neutral.
4 Give the command to enter the water.
5 When the divers are on the shot, you will already have drifted back to the buoy.
6 When you are clear of the divers and shot, move off.

Wind across current

1 You must choose to approach the buoy on its downwind side so that when you stop, the boat will be blown away from the divers and not across them.
2 Position the divers on the correct side of the boat before you begin to manoeuvre.
3 Motor at slow speed into the current, towards the buoy.
4 Stop before the buoy, put the engine into neutral.
5 Give the command to enter the water. When the divers have drifted to the shot, you will have been blown sideways away from the buoy.
6 When you are clear, reverse away.

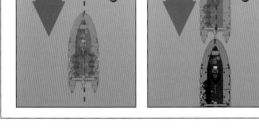

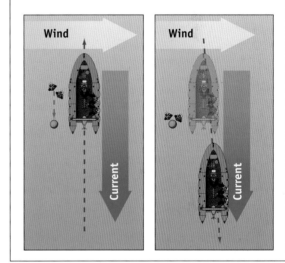

Key points to remember when dropping off divers

- Divers must have completed their buddy check and be sitting next to each other on the same side of the boat, before the final positioning of the boat.
- Engine must be in neutral, and forward movement of the boat must have stopped, before divers are given the go ahead to enter the water.
- Remember the wind and tide will continue to affect the boat when the engine is in neutral. Wind will tend to turn the boat side on to the wind.

- In most cases, wind will have a greater effect on the boat than current.
- In most cases, current will have a greater effect on divers in the water than wind.
- Any current can be detected by assessing which way the shot-line is being pulled by the water or better still by using a tidal indicator buoy attached to the shot-line buoy with a length of line. This will trail out in the direction of any current.

Dropping off divers

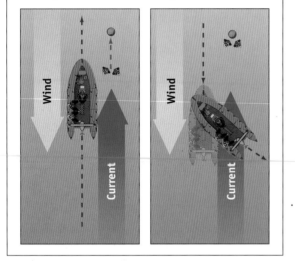

Wind against current
1 The wind is likely to affect the boat more than the current.
2 Motor at slow speed into wind, towards the buoy, so that it is on the same side of the boat as your divers.
3 Stop before the buoy, put the engine into neutral.
4 Give the command to enter the water.
5 When the divers have drifted to the shot, you will have been blown back downwind, and turned across the wind.
6 When you are clear, reverse away.

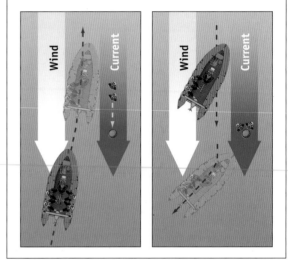

Wind and current in same direction
1 Motor at slow speed into the current, past the buoy, to drop your divers uptide of it as in the 'current, no wind' scenario, but angle the bows slightly in to the buoy, so that when you fall back, the wind will turn the boat's stern away from the buoy and divers.
2 Only engage gear to reverse away when you have drifted well clear of the divers and shot.

If you are not happy with any part of your approach to drop off divers, you should move away and begin again. It is easier to correct yourself by making a completely fresh approach, rather than trying to salvage a poor one.

In good sea conditions it is an option to tie off to a fixed buoy, drop your divers, and then release from the buoy. It is, however, good practice to keep the cover boat mobile during a dive so that if any divers surface unexpectedly or indicate an emergency, the boat can reach them as quickly as possible. As soon as you have divers in the water, remember to display your A-flag. Then, monitor the divers on the surface until they submerge. If your divers are using a surface marker buoy, you will be able to follow them during the dive. If you have more than one SMB to follow, keep them all in sight, even if this means motoring between them. Once you have lost sight of one

it may be more difficult to spot it again. If your divers are on a well-defined site such as a wreck you may not have an SMB to watch. Keep a lookout in all directions at all times – to achieve this ask two crewmembers to monitor the sea surface in opposite directions. Investigate all unusual things that you see. A distant diver on the surface may not be instantly recognisable as such and the longer they are left on the surface, the farther apart you will become. Patrol a largish area around the entry point and expected surfacing point of your divers. You should be monitoring any wind and tide and taking this into account when deciding where to expect your divers to surface. The use of delayed SMBs, deployed as soon as divers begin their ascent and therefore enter into the moving water column, reduces the chance of divers becoming separated from the boat.

Diver prepares to climb a hard boat ladder

Crew will need to help divers de-kit before they can get back into an inflatable

Picking up divers

If your divers surface using a shot-line, you will need to indicate to them to move away from it when you are ready to pick them up. Divers on the surface will not be stationary but the boat and the divers will be affected similarly by the tide, so you should approach slowly, and in a straight line, in to wind. Indicate which side of the boat you will be using for the pickup and ensure that there is a crewmember available to assist with de-kitting. Put the engine into neutral when the divers are level with the bow. Once the divers are ready to come aboard, it is the coxswain who confirms that the entry area is clear and divers can then enter the boat.

If you need to pick up divers near rocks, and they are not in distress, it is best to encourage them to swim out into open water. If there is a swell it will be particularly difficult for you to approach the rocks. If you do have to go in close, ask a crewmember to look out for submerged rocks from the bow.

If you cannot get near enough to the divers, or if swimming to the boat is a problem, use a throwing line to reach them (see *Throwing a line*, page 53). It is best to allow the divers to pull themselves hand over hand along the line to the boat, or for a crewmember to pull them in. It is uncomfortable and unsafe for a person on the surface to be towed by a boat, either holding onto the boat or holding onto a line, even when using an aqualung. It is too difficult for the boat to maintain the very slow speed needed to make this comfortable and safe. It may be possible to anchor the boat and drift backwards towards the divers, paying out the anchor line until you are close enough to reach them.

Recovering the boat

Recovering the boat

At the end of a boat trip, getting the boat back onto its trailer is a job for the whole team. If you are using a sheltered slipway in calm weather, there will be little pressure on you to recover the boat quickly except to free up the slip for other users. However if the weather conditions have deteriorated since launch then this routine task can become dangerous and it may be safer to anchor or moor the boat until conditions improve. If you are recovering a boat in breaking waves, it makes sense to keep out of the breakers until the team and the trailer are ready.

Preparing a trailer to recover a boat means organising someone to reverse it down to the water's edge, where it can be prepared for use. Unlock the winch reel and pay out the winching strap until it reaches beyond the back of the trailer. It is important at this stage to make sure that the strap runs the correct way through the roller, or bar, which will support the bow once the boat is on the trailer. If the winch is geared, set it to high gear to winch the boat onto the trailer. If winching becomes hard, change to low gear or have another person ready to help.

Inflatables

Inflatables can be recovered either by carrying them ashore or using a trailer. Carrying an inflatable ashore means that you will have to unload all the equipment first. The team can then carry the boat, with the engine in position if necessary. The grab lines running

A RIB will need little help to centre itself on the trailer once winching is underway

along the sides of inflatables are not usually structural. To lift a heavy boat it is better to use the solid grab handles provided.

To recover an inflatable onto a trailer, loosely attach the winch strap to the inflatable's secure fixing, usually a u-bolt at the bow. As winching begins the boat must be floated into position, centred over the trailer. With members of the team keeping the boat centred, to avoid any damage to tubes or hull, both trailer and boat can be pulled into shallower water, until the boat comes to rest on the trailer boards. Wind in the winch strap until the boat's bow is resting securely on the travelling support bar and lock off the winch.

RIBs and dories

RIBs and dories, because of their weight, are always recovered onto trailers. Depending on the slope of the slipway or shore, you will have to decide how far into the water to reverse the trailer. Depending on the type of hubs that the trailer has, it may be worth reducing corrosion of the wheel bearings by keeping them out of the water.

Once the trailer is in position, the divers and crew can bring the boat into position, lined up behind the trailer. It is usually not necessary to float a RIB or dory directly over the trailer. Most trailers set up for RIBs or dories are fitted with pivoting rollers or a swinging roller beam, which allows the winch to pull the boat up out of the water and onto the trailer. Once the boat is in position and the winch strap is attached to its secure fixing on the boat, usually the through-the-hull U-bolt at the bow, winching can begin. At the start, the divers and crew will need to help keep the boat in line with the trailer, but it will centre itself as it is pulled up out of the water.

Once the boat is loaded onto the trailer, do a final check to make sure that it is sitting correctly on the supports and that the winch is locked off so that the boat cannot move backwards. Making sure that no one is behind the trailer, and all are standing clear, the towing vehicle can pull the trailer clear of the water and out of the way of other users.

Once clear of the water and suitably parked, the boat should be allowed to drain to reduce stress on the hull from the weight of water inside it. Sloping ground, such as a slipway, is ideal for this and letting down the 'elephant's trunk' at the stern allows the boat to drain easily.

The boat and trailer can now be made ready for the road. Webbing straps fastened at the stern and amidships keep the boat securely in place. Check that the winch is still locked into position. As an extra safeguard you can fasten the boat to the trailer using the painter. If you use a boat cover, make sure that it is securely fastened into place. You must fix a suitable prop bag over the propeller (see *Trailing and the UK law*, page 76). To travel on a public road, a trailer light board is needed. Care must be taken when positioning the electrical cable that powers the lights - too little slack will mean that the plug is easily pulled out of the socket on the car when the cable extends during a turn, too much slack and the cable will be shredded by contact with the road.

Chapter two

Working with ropes

As a diver, you may have come across some quite specific uses of ropes underwater, but as a boat user you will almost inevitably handle rope on every trip that you make.

When choosing a rope for a particular job strength, handling characteristics and size must all be considered. Ropes are measured across their diameter in millimetres, at the widest part. If you are given a size in inches it is probably a measure of the circumference of the rope. Most ropes used on dive boats will be 10-20 mm in diameter, as this is a good size to handle and more than strong enough.

Choosing a rope

Choosing a rope

Spun, or hawser-laid, rope was the most commonly available type when ropes were made of natural fibres. It is made up of many thin yarns spun into thicker strands, which are in turn laid out together to make the rope. The twist used to make the yarn into strands, and the twist used to make the strands into the rope are in opposite directions and this is what holds the rope together. Most spun rope is three-stranded and the strands are laid right handed: if you hold the rope so that it points away from you the strands go to the right.

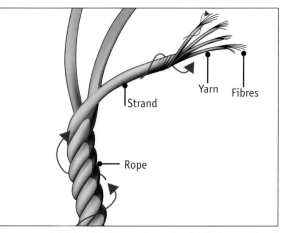

A right-hand laid rope is made of left-hand twisted strands of right-hand spun yarn

Factors to consider when choosing a rope

- Strength – the safe working load of a rope is its breaking strength divided by a safety factor of four for synthetic ropes or six for natural fibres. A knot reduces the strength by 50 per cent. A splice reduces the strength by 12 per cent.
- Elasticity – a useful property in mooring lines, not so useful where a standing line is required.
- Cost – for one-off uses such as surveys and salvage work, low-cost ropes may do. Otherwise it may be worth paying more for the rope best suited to the job.
- Handling – a rope that is frequently used must be pleasant to handle.
- Stowability – consider the stiffness of a rope if you have to stow it in a small space.

Talking about ropes

Bend – a way of tying the ends of two lines together

Bight – the middle of a line, a loop or curve in a line

Flake – to lay down a rope so that it pays out freely

Heat-seal – to melt and fuse the ends of a synthetic rope, to prevent it unravelling

Hitch – a knot used to secure a line to a ring or post

Knot – a way of forming a noose, a fixed loop or a stopper in the end of a line

Lay – the direction in which the strands of a rope are twisted

Line – a rope used for a particular purpose

Pay out – to let out a chain or rope

Seizing – a lashing for holding two ropes or parts of a rope together

Standing part – the main part of the line, as distinguished from the bight, on which the knot is tied, and the end, with which the knot is tied

Stop – to lash temporarily

Whipping – a small lashing of sail twine to prevent the end of a rope unravelling

Other types of rope include cable-laid (three strands laid up, left-handed), shroud-laid (four strands laid up, right-handed around a heart), plaited and many types of core/cover ropes. Plaited ropes have increased flexibility and a square profile that should not kink. But they cannot be spliced together, so they are usually knotted, which reduces their strength. Core/cover ropes are made from a variety of different cores – 3-strand, braided or parallel fibres – covered with a variety of different plaited covers. Some can be spliced, some cannot.

The characteristics of a rope depend on the fibres that it is made of, as well as its construction. Rope made from natural fibres such as hemp or sisal seems hairy because the ends of the short natural fibres protrude all over its surface and these help such ropes to hold knots well. However, natural ropes have some disadvantages; when wet, they tend to swell, rot and freeze among other things. So although they sink when wet, which is useful to divers, natural fibre ropes have largely been replaced with synthetic ones.

In synthetic ropes, the fibres run the length of the rope, giving a smooth appearance. But such ropes, although pleasant to handle, may not hold knots as well as natural ones. They can be given a hairy surface by shortening the length of the fibres used. Synthetic ropes have high strength-to-weight ratios and require less care than natural ropes and so they are practical for use in small boats.

Nylon, polyester and polypropylene are the main fibres used to make synthetic ropes. High modulus polyethylene, aramid and liquid crystal polymers are more recent additions to the range. Nylon is a high-stretch, high-strength fibre and it has good weather and abrasion resistance. It is particularly suited to applications needing elasticity, such as towing or mooring lines.

Polyester is a low-stretch, high-strength fibre making strong ropes that are less elastic than nylon. It also has good weather and abrasion resistance and is often used to cover marine ropes.

Polypropylene has about 60 per cent of the strength of nylon or polyester. Its low melting point means that it is not suitable for use where high friction is generated. However, polypropylene rope floats and is cheap, which makes it popular for many boating applications.

High modulus polyethylene is a very low-stretch, very high-strength fibre – weight-for-weight it is the strongest fibre in the world. Aramid, while similarly strong and low stretch, has poor abrasion resistance and is affected by ultra-violet light so it tends to be used in the core of a rope with a polyester cover. It also has a tendency to sudden failure. Liquid crystal polymers have almost perfect characteristics, but again are sensitive to UV light and so are used within a cover. The superb performance of such fibres is probably of more use in a racing yacht than a diving boat.

The type of rope that you choose depends upon its use

Using ropes

Using ropes

Ropes have many purposes on a small boat. Generally they are used as links between objects and so they have to be fastened by knotting. There is a relatively small selection of knots likely to be used on a diving boat and we will take a look at them here. In general, the simpler the knot, the more likely it is to be harmful to the rope as the tension is spread over fewer turns. Knots that use more turns will be less harmful, as the increased friction will absorb the load more gradually and jam less readily. A knot that is strong under tension may not be secure when the load is released. A secure knot will hold well under varying conditions.

Ways of tying ropes can be subdivided into knots, bends and hitches depending on their purpose. Let's take a look.

Knots

These are ways of forming a noose, a fixed loop or a stopper in the end of a line.

Bowline

This is a secure knot that will not slip or jam and is easy to undo. It forms a loop, or eye, in a rope. It can be used to make a loop threaded through a ring or with another bowline in another rope to join two ropes together, when a shot line or mooring line needs extending, for example.

To tie a bowline, form a small loop in the standing part of the rope, with the shorter end on top. Bring the end of the rope up through the loop, pass it behind the standing part and back down through the loop. Holding the end against the side of the loop, pull the standing part to tighten. This is a right-handed bowline. If the end part of the rope lies outside the loop, the knot is a left-handed bowline: in practice this works as well as the right-handed knot.

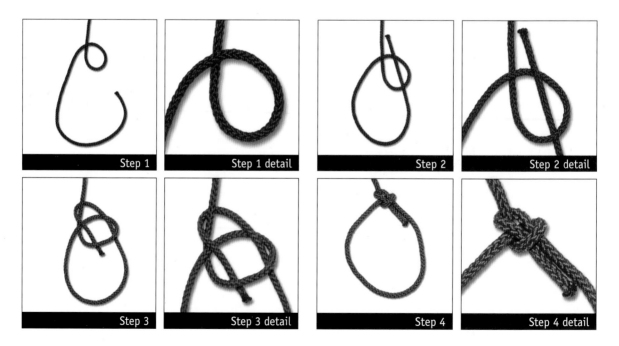

Step 1 | Step 1 detail | Step 2 | Step 2 detail

Step 3 | Step 3 detail | Step 4 | Step 4 detail

Reef knot

This knot is used to join two pieces of rope of equal diameter and type together that will remain under permanent tension. For example to enclose or bind something, such as a bundle, where it is tied with two ends of the same line. It can be used when securing the boat cover to the trailer, for example. It tends to slip if ropes of different diameters and materials are used. It should never be used to join two separate lengths of rope together. The reef knot consists of two overhand knots tied on top of each other, one left-handed and one right-handed. Otherwise, it becomes a granny knot which will slip or jam.

Reef knot   Granny knot

Figure-of-eight knot

This is a simple, useful stopper knot that does not jam hard as a simple overhand knot would. It can be used to stop a line from fraying or to prevent a line passing through a hole. A figure-of-eight knot is useful for creating a loop in

a line, to clip a buoy to at the top of a shotline for example. Double up the standing part of your line at the point that you want to create the loop, allowing enough doubled up line to comfortably tie the knot. Use the loop end of the doubled up line as the free end of rope and tie a figure of eight knot. This will be easy to undo even if it is put under considerable load.

Bends

These are ways of tying the ends of two lines together.

Sheet bend

This knot is traditionally used for joining two lines of different diameters and materials, but with modern ropes they can slip when the strain is released so they are not

Sheet bend   Double sheet bend

Sheet bend with a slip

Figure-of-eight knot   Double figure-of-eight knot

Hitches

suitable for extending the length of shot lines.

Start by taking a bight in the thicker of the two lines. Pass the thinner line up through the loop, from the underneath, around the back and across the front of the loop, under its own standing part. If the first line is very stiff, taking an additional turn around the neck of the bight to make a double sheet bend will increase the security of the knot.

Hitches

These are knots used to secure a line to a ring or post.

Two half-hitches

These are often used to temporarily hitch a line to a ring or post, such as when mooring to a quay. The two hitches should be tied in the same direction.

Two half-hitches

Round turn and two half-hitches

This is a far better hitch, as the round turn gives extra friction and reduces wear on the rope. The extra friction means the knot remains fast under varying rope tensions, for example when a moored boat constantly jerks on the line. Also, the round turn protects the hitches from tightening, so this knot remains easy to undo. To tie, pass the line over the rail twice and then tie two half-hitches.

Round turn and two half-hitches

Clove hitch

This can be used to make a painter fast to a post or railing, but it relies on a constant tension on the line to keep it secure, otherwise it works loose. To tie in a quick way, over a bollard, throw a single hitch over the bollard keeping the loose end under the standing part. You can hold the strain using the friction of this first loop. Then throw a second loop above the first, again keeping the loose end under the standing part. Tighten the knot.

To tie onto a railing, pass the free end around the rail and bring it over and to the right of the standing part. Pass it over the rail again, to the right of the first turn, and bring the end between the two turns (see picture series opposite).

Anchor bend

This can be used to attach a rope to a ring or handle, on a shot weight or anchor, for example. Take the end of the line twice through the ring, keeping the loops relaxed. Pass the end of the line behind the standing part and through the loops you have just made. Pull tight. Secure with two half-hitches, by passing it through a lay or using seizing.

Splicing

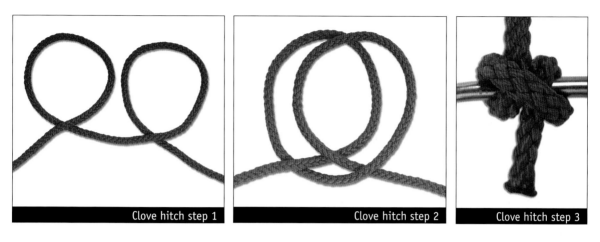

Clove hitch step 1

Clove hitch step 2

Clove hitch step 3

Anchor bend

Belaying onto a mooring cleat

Slips

It is easy to improve the speed with which knots can be undone by finishing them with a slip. This means taking the end back through the last part of the knot so that it only needs to be pulled to undo the knot (refer to sheet bend with slip).

Belaying

Boats may have cleats for tying off lines. Belaying means making a line fast by winding it around a cleat. To do this take a turn around the cleat, leading the standing part to the far end of the cleat. Then lay on several figure-of-eight turns, finishing with a locking turn, where the end passes underneath the turn, if you wish the line to remain fast for some time. If the belay is temporary, and attended by someone, you may choose to leave out the locking turn in order to be able to free the line quickly.

Working with ropes **49**

Eye Splice

Splicing

Knotting a rope puts an uneven strain on it and weakens it because of the sharp bends the rope is put through to form the knot. The alternative, a splice, is a permanent join between two ropes that retains most of their original strength. Splicing two ropes together keeps the fibres parallel, which allows them to share the load evenly.

Step by step eye splice

This splice can be used to attach a line to a fitting, for example to the anchor, to a u-bolt, or to a karabiner.

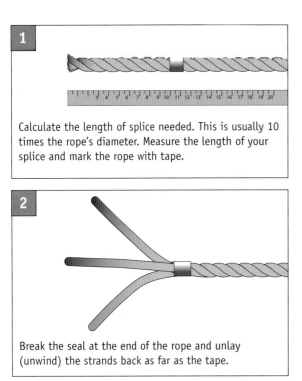

Calculate the length of splice needed. This is usually 10 times the rope's diameter. Measure the length of your splice and mark the rope with tape.

Break the seal at the end of the rope and unlay (unwind) the strands back as far as the tape.

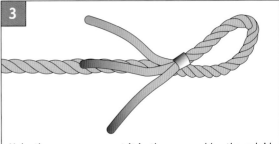

Make the eye as you want it in the rope and lay the unlaid strands in a fan over the standing part of the rope.

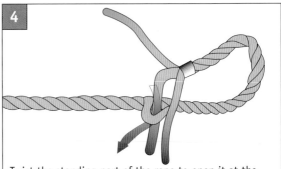

Twist the standing part of the rope to open it at the point where you want the eye to close. Insert the middle strand of the fan into the opening at right angles to the standing part and pointing away from the eye. It is helpful to use a tool to keep the rope open, such as a marlinspike or a fid (not shown).

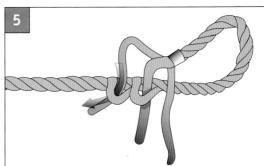

As your next strand, choose the one lying on the inside of the eye. This may lie above or below the first strand, depending on how you formed your eye. If it lies above, tuck it under the strand in the standing part that is above the first tuck. If it lies below, tuck it under the strand in the standing part that is below the first tuck.

6

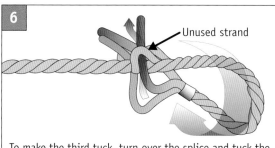

Unused strand

To make the third tuck, turn over the splice and tuck the remaining unlaid strand under the strand in the standing part that lies between the two you have already used.

7

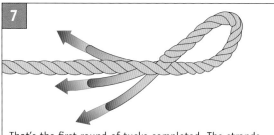

That's the first round of tucks completed. The strands are secure so you can remove the tape. Pull the strands individually to tighten the splice and make the throat of the eye.

8

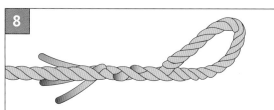

Complete the splice by making tucks with alternate strands, one by one. Work around the rope to avoid confusion and keep the splice tight.

9

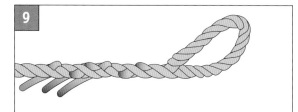

When the splice is long enough, you will need to taper the splice. Stop one strand first. Continue for another tuck with the next one and a further tuck with the last.

10

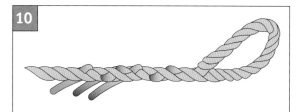

The unlaid strands will all exit from the rope on the same side. Trim them to within 2mm of the splice with a hot knife. Do not damage the standing part of the rope while doing this. The melted ends should retract into the splice.

An eye splice on a painter

Tips for a good splice

- Five tucks is the absolute minimum for a secure splice.
- Ideally, the length of unlaid strands should be about ten times the diameter of the rope, for example for a 10mm rope use 10cm unlaid strands.
- Twist each strand before making a tuck to maintain the structure of the rope.
- To finish off a splice, roll it between your hands, or underfoot, to bed in all the tucks properly and smooth the rope.

Short Splice

The short splice

This is a way of joining two ropes together, but it increases the diameter of the rope at the join, which may affect how the rope runs in a fairlead for example.

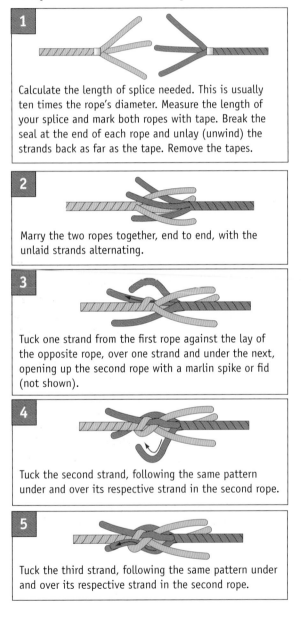

1

Calculate the length of splice needed. This is usually ten times the rope's diameter. Measure the length of your splice and mark both ropes with tape. Break the seal at the end of each rope and unlay (unwind) the strands back as far as the tape. Remove the tapes.

2

Marry the two ropes together, end to end, with the unlaid strands alternating.

3

Tuck one strand from the first rope against the lay of the opposite rope, over one strand and under the next, opening up the second rope with a marlin spike or fid (not shown).

4

Tuck the second strand, following the same pattern under and over its respective strand in the second rope.

5

Tuck the third strand, following the same pattern under and over its respective strand in the second rope.

6

Do the same for the first, second and third unlaid strands from the second rope, by repeating steps 3, 4 and 5 on the other half of the splice.

7

Ease all the tucked strands from both ropes into place, putting the same tension on each one so that the join between ropes feels firm not floppy.

8

Following the pattern established by the first sequence of tucks (steps 4 to 7), begin to repeat the tucking process.

9

Continue to work around the second sequence of tucks.

10

Ease the second round of tucks into place, putting the same tension on each one so that the splice looks even.

11

Repeat the tucking process for the third and final time.

12

Trim the remaining unlaid strands to within 2mm of the splice with a hot knife. Do not damage the standing part of the rope while doing this. The melted ends should retract into the splice. Roll the splice between your hands to help this process.

Stowing rope

Lines on a boat need to be kept neatly stowed to prevent tangling and ensure ease of use when required. If you have the space, the easiest way to stow a frequently used line such as the main anchor line is to flake it into a container. A tub or a crate can be used for this and the line is simply poured into the container, in reverse order. As it goes in, so it should come out. Remember to start flaking with the end that you do not want to pull out first.

On larger boats, ropes that need to be paid out quickly may be kept on a revolving reel or drum. Such lines will normally be recovered using a winch and may be loaded back onto the reel later.

Coiling is the best method of storing less frequently used lines. To coil without kinking you must take into account the lay of the rope. For a rope with a right hand lay, hold the end of the line in your left hand. Draw in and coil the rope clockwise with your right hand, giving it a clockwise twist with your thumb and forefinger before making each coil. This will send any tangles down the rope to the free end. It may be necessary to shake out the free end every now and then. Keep the coils the same size as each other.

To stow the finished coil take the free end in your right hand, wrap it round the coil a couple of times about a third of the way down, pass the free end through the top half of the coil and pull it tight. Hanging up the coil helps drying and this benefits the rope.

Maintenance of rope

Ropes suffer from wear when in use and this can weaken them considerably. Well-used synthetic ropes may appear furry: this hairy surface, in fact, helps to protect against further abrasion. However, they should be inspected regularly along their whole length to check for cuts and abrasions. It is often the end of a rope that suffers and this can be trimmed to give a good end again. A worn line can always be downgraded to a use that puts it under a smaller load.

Knots jammed into a line will also weaken it; they should be undone and, provided no damage is done to the rope, its original strength is restored.

Synthetic ropes can be stored wet without adverse effects. Like all diving equipment, there is no problem using natural ropes in the sea, it is the drying out afterwards that causes problems. The resulting salt crystals will affect the life of ropes, so they should be soaked in fresh water at least at the end of each season.

Throwing a line

It is useful to be able to throw a rope in a straight line, whether to a person on a quay as part of the mooring process or to a person in the water as part of a rescue. To do this, coil the rope in your left hand, as if you are going to store it. Take a few loops of the coil into your right hand, keeping the free end towards your fingertips and keeping your left arm outstretched, fingers unclenched. Throw the coils in your right hand directly at the recipient. Their weight will make the coil in your left hand feed out smoothly. Do not forget to hold, or tie off, the inboard end of the line before throwing.

Throwing lines designed for life-saving purposes are often kept stuffed carefully into a lightweight, tubular nylon bag which is weighted at the closed end. The bag is just the right size to hold the rope fairly snugly and is closed loosely around a protruding free end. To use this type of throwing line you simply hold the free end, and throw the bag at the recipient. The weight of the rope and bag make it easy to throw the rope accurately, and the line pays out as it is needed.

Anchoring systems

Anchoring

The anchor is an essential part of any boat's safety equipment. Its main use is to keep the boat in one place, either to park or to prevent the boat drifting away in an emergency. The anchor can also be used to keep the bows head on to the waves, if you are stationary. However, it is always good practice for the dive boat to remain mobile during any dive.

The main parts of a small boat anchoring system are the anchor itself, a short length of chain, a rope and a buoy. There are different designs of anchor (see *The merits of different anchors*, page 57) and they are available in different weights. A common fault is to choose too small an anchor for a small boat. A boat of 3 to 4 metres in length should have an anchor of 5 kilograms. Boats more than 5 metres long will need up to 10 kilograms to hold them in a moderate sea. In rougher weather the strain on the anchor increases. You cannot readily change your anchor to cope with this, but you can let out more line to help the anchor hold fast.

Understanding how an anchor holds will help you to choose the right equipment for your boat and to anchor proficiently in all circumstances. Whichever type of anchor you choose, it will work best if the pull on it from the boat is close to horizontal, spreading the load over an increased area of sea bed. To achieve this an anchor must be given what is called plenty of 'scope' – that is, plenty of line to allow the anchor to lie horizontally.

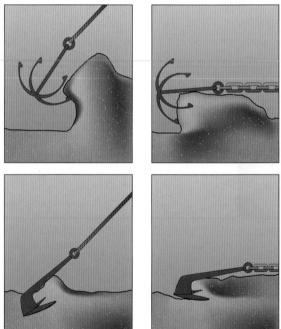

Insecure anchor holds poorly   Secure anchor holds well

The anchor stock must lie along the sea bed if it is to hold well. The chain helps ensure this

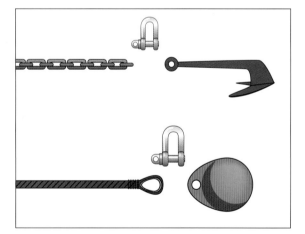

Anchor components

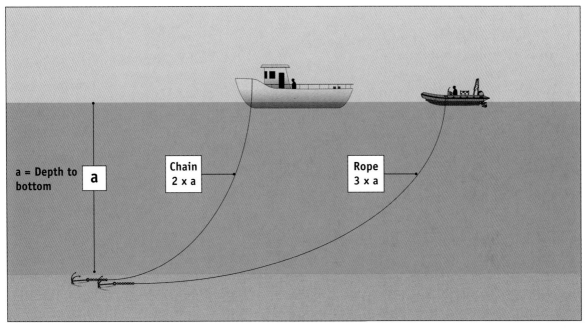

a = Depth to bottom

a

Chain 2 x a

Rope 3 x a

You can calculate the theoretical amount of chain or warp needed to anchor in a certain depth

Larger boats use galvanised steel chain as their anchor line. It is attached to the anchor with a galvanised steel shackle and let out or hauled in using a winch. In theory, to anchor with chain you will need a scope of 12 times the square root of the depth of water that you are in. Chain is relatively heavy and helps keep the anchor lying parallel to the sea bed, so you need relatively little of it.

Smaller boats tend to use a short length of chain – when compared to the overall length of the anchor line – to pull down on the anchor. Remember, any upward pull will make an anchor less effective. Three to four metres of a short link galvanised chain of 6 to 8 millimetres in diameter would be ideal. This can be attached to the anchor at one end, and the anchor rope at the other, by galvanised shackles. When attaching the rope you can either use an anchor bend or, better still, an eye splice (see *Working with ropes*, page 50).

Any shackles used as part of an anchoring system should be put in place, tightened and then wired to prevent the shackle-bolt becoming unscrewed during use. Shackles have a hole in the flat end of the bolt. Put a short length of wire through this hole, twist it together, wrap it around one of the sides of the U-shaped shackle and then twist it together again. This will prevent any vibration shaking the bolt undone during use.

Anchor rope should be chosen for its handling properties, its stowability and its ability to be spliced. A rope of 10 to 12 mm in diameter is suitable for use on small dive boats. In theory, when using rope as an anchor warp, a RIB would need a scope of 20 times the square root of the depth of water. The combination of a short chain and rope is less efficient at keeping the anchor horizontal than chain alone, so you need more of it. However, a good rule of thumb for a dive boat is to have an anchor line that is three times the maximum depth that you anticipate anchoring in. For a RIB, 60 metres of rope with 3 to 4 metres of chain would allow you to anchor in depths of up to 20 metres. In bad weather it may be necessary to let out more line to hold your position.

Tripping line

If you anchor in an area where the anchor is likely to get stuck on the sea bed, you can use a tripping line to help retrieve the anchor. This is a second line and buoy attached to a point on the base of the shaft of the anchor. By pulling on the base of the shaft it is often possible to pull clear of a jam. A tripping line must not disturb the anchor's position at rest, as it is not intended to take any of the weight of the anchor until it is recovered, so it needs to be relatively long. However, it can be a hazard on the surface and should be weighted a few metres from the buoy.

Types of anchor

Different shapes of anchor have different holding capabilities on different sea beds. Rocky reefs and boulders provide hard surfaces with many cavities and overhangs. To hold here an anchor must hook in. Sand and mud are unstable, moving substrates and to hold here an anchor must dig in.

There are five basic anchor types: fisherman's or Admiralty pattern; CQR or plough; Danforth; Bruce; and grapnel. Admiralty pattern anchors are not used by the type of boats that are discussed in this book.

Setting up a tripping line

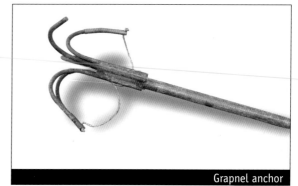

Grapnel anchor

The merits of different anchors suitable for use on small diving boats

CQR
For: high holding-to-weight ratio
Against: hard to stow,
moving parts can break
Good for: mud

Danforth
For: good holding-to-weight ratio,
stows flat
Against: moving parts can jam,
hard to break out of mud
Good for: sand

Bruce
For: high holding-to-weight ratio,
lighter than a CQR in relation to its holding power,
no moving parts
Against: difficult to stow
Good for: mud

Folding grapnel
For: easy to stow
Against: can fold up in use if not assembled properly,
too light to hold if not hooked in,
poor on sand and mud,
not suitable as a main anchor
Good for: boulders

Stowing the anchor

Stowing the anchor

A boat anchor must be ready to use at all times. Dive boats tend to have limited deck and storage space so it is tempting, but unwise, to let the anchor disappear underneath everything else.

The anchor should be attached to the bow of the boat. Then, when it is deployed, it will hold the boat into the waves or current. Also, the bow of the boat tends to move up and down the most and is therefore uncomfortable for passengers and dangerous for delicate diving equipment, but provides ample storage space for the anchor.

If an anchor rope and chain is left loose on the deck it would soon be unusable, so it is usually stowed in a locker, bin or basket, or on a reel. The inboard end of the anchor warp should be attached to a secure point in the boat with a way of releasing it quickly. The secure point could be either a special fitting on the deck or through the hull at the bows. Most RIBs have a through-the-hull U-bolt positioned at the bows below the tubes. The painter – a length of rope not long enough to reach the propeller that is used for mooring purposes – is usually attached to this U-bolt. The painter may have a stainless-steel karabiner spliced to its free end.

When you have deployed the anchor you may choose to make a loop in the anchor line at the surface, using a double figure-of-eight knot (see *Tying a figure-of-eight*, page 47), and clip the painter to the line. This ensures that the jerking on the anchor is taken by a strong point on the hull. Let the remaining anchor line lie loose beside the taut painter and secure its end inboard to prevent it tumbling into the water.

The anchor rope should also be attached to a large buoy – 50 centimetres in diameter, for example – so that if you need to release the boat from the anchor quickly you do not need to waste time by pulling the anchor in, but you can just throw the remaining rope and buoy overboard. The buoy means that you will be able to find and retrieve the anchor when you have time.

How to stow the anchor

1. Attach the inboard end of the line to a secure point in the boat using a quick release fixing
2. Attach the buoy close to the end of the line
3. Place the container in a suitable place at the bow
4. Flake the line into a container, beginning with the inboard end
5. Continue flaking the chain into the container, on top of the rope
6. Stow the anchor securely in or near the container. Ensure that the anchor flukes cannot harm the divers and crew or the boat
7. Do not cover the anchor with any other equipment

Deploying the anchor

Before you anchor, make sure that you know which way any wind and current are moving, as they will influence the final position of the boat relative to the anchor.

You will also need to prepare the anchor. Before you start, ask someone to make sure that the anchor is ready for use and attached to the boat.

Having decided where you want to be, approach the position into the wind or tide, whichever is having the most effect on the boat, and pass slowly over your ideal

Preparing the anchor

Ready to drop anchor

Paying out the chain

anchoring spot. Come to a standstill about one boat length past your spot. Put the engine into neutral and as the boat begins to drop back, deploy the anchor. Your backward movement will prevent the anchor, chain and warp getting tangled on each other by keeping them stretched out. Allow the rope to move quickly and freely out of its container until you feel it hit the bottom. As you continue to drift backwards, allow the rope to pay out until you have paid out the correct amount to warp for the depth of water that you are in. Fasten the inboard end to the secure fitting on the boat. When you are sure that the anchor is holding securely, you can stop the engine. If there is no wind or current, you will need to go astern at slow speed to move the boat backwards.

By paying out the line in a free-flowing but controlled way, allowing the movement of the boat to straighten it out as you go, you will avoid a heap of anchor, chain and warp on the sea bed, which would not hold well. However, keeping too much tension on the warp during the anchoring process will prevent the anchor reaching the sea bed and positioning itself properly.

Remember that the boat is only attached to the sea bed at the bow. Any change in wind or tide will swing you around in an arc. It is possible that this will dislodge the anchor, especially in rough seas. You will need to allow enough room for the boat to swing at anchor when you choose your anchoring spot. All other boats in the vicinity will also swing around, but different sizes of boat may respond to wind and tide at different speeds.

Before anchoring consider the following:

- Select your anchorage from the chart on the basis of depth of water at low tide, type of holding ground, wind direction and swell direction
- Be aware of your environment. Do not anchor in places where you might damage corals and other marine life

- Do not anchor near moorings – you may foul ground chains
- Do not anchor in channels or fairways
- Do not anchor near other craft
- Allow enough space for the vessel to swing with the wind and tide

Retrieving the anchor

Retrieving the anchor

Before retrieving the anchor you must start the engine. Then you can disconnect the anchor warp from the boat and begin to pull it in. You will be pulling in the direction of the lie. If you motor ahead slowly in the same direction you will help to relieve the strain, but if you overrun the line you risk entangling it in the propeller.

As you retrieve the warp, flake it back into the container. When the rope becomes vertical in the water, the anchor should break free. If it fails to, then motoring over it and pulling in the opposite direction may help to free it. A tripping line would pull on the anchor in a more effective way, but it needs to be set up in advance and it doubles the amount of lines to be handled when deploying the anchor.

If all else fails, you will have to leave the anchor in place and return to free it later. You could ask a pair of divers to free it when they are ready to enter the water again. It may be that the tide has turned since you anchored, and when it turns again the anchor may come free. It is not advisable to send divers down immediately after a dive, as they are likely to be short of safe bottom time and dive gas. They will also probably be cold and tired if they have dived already. If the tide has turned, conditions underwater may not be favourable.

Setting up a shot-line

Shot-lines provide a marked entry and exit point for a dive, a direct route to the dive site and security for the descent and ascent phases of the dive. Your boat's anchor cannot substitute for the shot, because to anchor effectively an anchor line must allow the chain to lie horizontally along the sea bed. A shot-line should be as near vertical as possible to give divers the shortest route to the underwater dive site. Also, it is good practice to keep the cover boat mobile during a dive, so an important part of a dive boat's kit is a separate shot-line.

A weight, line, buoy and smaller tide buoy can be made into a shot-line

The simplest shot line consists of a buoy, a line and a shot weight. A top-tensioned shot, where the line runs through a loop on the connection to the buoy and is tensioned by a counterweight, is more complex to set up but has the advantage of rising and falling with the tide. It is most practical to store the shot-line in a container, such as a plastic bin.

You can shorten a shot by coiling the excess line

Keeping the line flaked into a container means the line pays out quickly as the shot descends

Setting up a shot-line

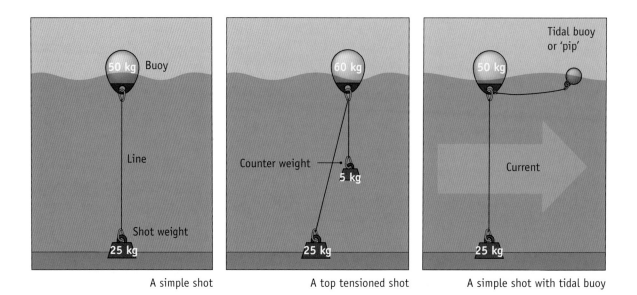

A simple shot   A top tensioned shot   A simple shot with tidal buoy

The line itself needs to be easy to handle if it has to be pulled up after every dive. Rope which has a diameter of 10 to 12 mm is ideal. The length of a fixed shot should be the depth of the water plus a few metres. A top-tensioned shot needs a few extra metres to form the overlap at the top.

The buoy should have 50 per cent more buoyancy than all of the weight attached to it. This will include the sinker weight, the counterweight if used, the line itself, and any aqualung sets needed for decompression. In any case, it should not have less than 50 kg buoyancy.

The weight needs to be heavy enough to stay put in a tide or current but not so heavy that it is difficult to recover: 15 to 25 kg is sufficient in most cases. When wreck diving, a grapnel makes a good sinker as it is easily secured in the wreckage by the first pair of divers and released by the last pair. A counterweight for a top-tensioned shot should be about 5 kg. However, the main shot weight will have to be heavier than 25 kg to counteract the counterweight. It is quickest to join the parts of the shot-line together with karabiners, tied or more securely spliced onto the various items.

If you plan to use a fixed shot-line you will need to prepare the shot in advance using a line of suitable length.

If, when the shot is deployed, there is some surplus line, it is best tidied away at the top of the shot. A good option is to attach a small buoy to the free end and let the line trail out on the surface. This gives you a tide buoy, sometimes referred to as a tidal pip, showing you what the current is doing on the surface. The direction in which the buoy and line stream away from the shot is the direction of the current. As the current slackens, the tide buoy's line will become less taut. Other options for tidying the line include: coiling it, knotting it and clipping the coil to the buoy; or using a chain sennet or knotted sheepshank, which shortens it and prevents entanglement.

Ways to find the buoyancy of a buoy

- Check the markings on the buoy
- Fill an old buoy of the same size with water, counting how many litres you put in. Each litre of water gives one kilogram of buoyancy.
- Carry out a test, in shallow water, attaching known weights to the buoy until it sinks.

Making a chain sennet

A chain sennet is a useful way of shortening the loose end of a rope. Because of its bulk, the chain remains untangled even when put into moving water so it is a practical way of shortening the line at the top of a shot. Throw or tie a loop at the point where you would like the chain sennet to start, then pull a loop of the next nearest part of the free end of rope through the starting loop to create another loop in the chain. Continue this process until you have shortened the line. Feed the free end through the last loop and pull tight to secure. When you want to undo the chain sennet, undo the free end and pull.

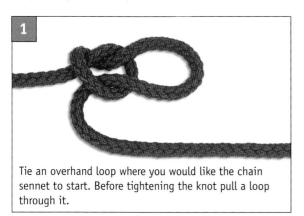

Tie an overhand loop where you would like the chain sennet to start. Before tightening the knot pull a loop through it.

Pull a second loop through the first loop.

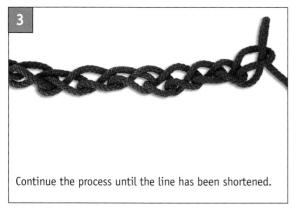

Continue the process until the line has been shortened.

Feed the free end through the last loop to secure.

Chapter three
Engines and trailers

The majority of club dive boats in the UK are powered by outboard engines. This section is designed to give people with little knowledge of outboard engines some insights into choosing and using an engine, including some basic fault finding that can be carried out at sea. Outboard engines today are efficient and reliable machines that will give many years of service if properly looked after.

Outboard engines

Outboard engines

Two types of outboards are commonly available: two-stroke and four-stroke petrol engines. Engine size is quoted as their horsepower, or hp, and varies from just a few hp to several hundred. The two-stroke engine is relatively simple and therefore cheap to build. It is easy to maintain, light in weight and compact. Four-stroke engines, however, use less fuel and oil than two-strokes of comparable power and they are quieter. Diesel outboards are available but they are outside the scope of this book.

The choice of engine depends upon the size and design of the boat and the type of boating that you expect to do. It is more economical, in terms of both fuel consumption and engine wear, to use a large enough engine to power your boat with ease. A larger engine will allow you to throttle back once you are planing, giving fuel economy without losing speed. Also, you will have power in reserve for an emergency.

But an engine can also be too big for a boat. Most boat manufacturers recommend a maximum engine size for their boats, and a maximum load. Remember when calculating load that each diver has about half a person's weight of kit on board too.

All outboards have a common set of controls. Smaller engines are started using a recoil pull cord and are tilted into and out of the water manually. There is a tilt lock which is used to lock the engine into the lowered or raised position. This must be engaged when you use reverse gear to prevent the engine leg moving up out of the water. There is a gear lever at one side of the engine casing with three positions: forward gear, neutral, and reverse gear.

Larger engines – from 40 to 50 hp upwards – tend to use an electric start, as their compression is far too great to start them manually, except perhaps in an emergency. They also have electric tilt. This can be operated remotely from the console, which is useful when driving the boat, or by a switch on the engine's bottom cowling, which is useful when the boat is on the trailer. Boat electrics are powered by a battery, which is charged up when the engine

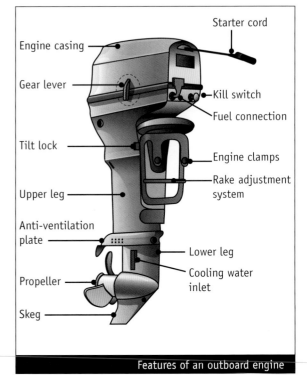

Features of an outboard engine

Engine casing
Starter cord
Gear lever
Kill switch
Fuel connection
Tilt lock
Engine clamps
Rake adjustment system
Upper leg
Anti-ventilation plate
Lower leg
Cooling water inlet
Propeller
Skeg

is running. Keeping the electrics dry on an inflatable is difficult, whereas on a RIB it is easier to position the battery out of the way in a locker.

All outboards have an easily accessible stop button, and many have a kill switch. This is a clip that holds the stop button in position but is fastened to the coxswain using a lanyard of some kind. If pulled, for example by the person falling overboard, the clip releases, the button closes and the engine stops.

Generally speaking, inflatable boats use tiller steering, which is available on engines up to 40 or 50 hp. Their portable nature means they cannot easily accommodate all of the apparatus associated with remote steering systems. And a coxswain sitting next to the engine on an inflatable boat has good visibility. RIBs, however, are better suited to a forward console with a wheel using remote cable steering and remote gear change and tilt controls. In most cases, if you sat next to the engine in a RIB you would have poor visibility due to the shape of the bow and the way the boat rides through the water. The rigid hull makes it easier to position the cables, which need to be firmly fixed to eliminate any cable movement.

When choosing your outboard engine the first thing you need to know is the transom depth of the boat. Outboards are available with long, extra-long or standard shafts. Long-shaft and extra-long shaft engines are required if the transom is 51 centimetres and 63 centimetres deep, respectively. Standard-shaft engines are appropriate where the transom does not exceed 38 centimetres. When the engine is fitted correctly, the anti-ventilation plate on the lower leg of the engine should be just above the water when you are on the plane. If it is much lower it will cause drag, and reduce efficiency and speed. If it is higher, the propeller will suffer from ventilation. This means air is drawn in from the surface to around the moving propeller, which slows the boat down. Ventilation can be recognised by a rapid rise in engine note and unless you throttle back you risk damaging the engine by running it at excessively high revs. This is not the same as cavitation (see *Propellers*, page 68).

Another variable to be adjusted on an outboard is the rake. This is the angle between the engine leg and the transom. The correct rake ensures that the boat is in the best position in the water, when under power. Too much forward tilt will make the boat plough into the sea. If the tilt is set too far aft, the boat will squat.

On engines with hydraulic tilt mechanisms, the correct rake is achieved using tilt and there is often a gauge to show what degree of tilt is in use. Engines with manual tilt mechanisms have a separate, manual rake adjustment system.

Any outboard needs to be securely attached to its boat. Smaller engines can be clamped to the transom with thumbscrews. Fixing the clamp buckles together means that they cannot unscrew but it is wise to use a wire strop attached to a secure fixing point on the boat to prevent the engine disappearing overboard. The torque that an outboard generates tends to twist the engine away from the boat. Larger engines need to be bolted through the transom. Bolts also give a measure of security from theft, especially if fitted with a bolt lock.

Too much forward tilt makes the boat plough in

Too much aft tilt causes the boat to squat

A correctly aligned engine positions the boat properly in the water

Propellers

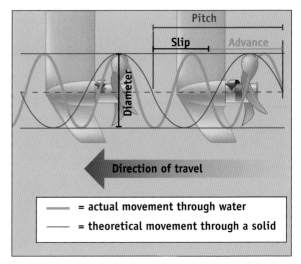

Propellers

An outboard engine's transmission system converts the high-speed rotation of the engine's crankshaft into useful thrust generated by spinning the propeller, which is used to move the boat through the water. It is important to have the right propeller for the job. It needs to match the boat, engine and gearbox. While engine manufacturers fit a standard propeller to their engines, they do recognise the fact that different uses need different propellers and offer a range of alternatives. An engine dealer will be able to help you choose a good propeller for your particular set-up, but there are a few things that you need to know first.

A propeller looks simple – but the science of propellers is remarkably complex. There are three ways of thinking about how a propeller works and each explains some, if not all, of its properties. It can be thought of as a screw winding its way onto a bolt, as a pump pushing a column of water out behind it, or as an aircraft wing depending for its lift on the relative speeds of the water flowing on each side of the blades.

Thinking of a propeller as a screw would work well if the propeller worked in a solid medium, but in water the analogy falls down. However, this theory explains some of the terminology used. The pitch of a propeller is the distance it would move forwards in one revolution if it were moving through a solid. A propeller does not move that far in one revolution in water. The distance that it actually moves is called the advance and the difference between pitch and advance is the slip. The pitch of a propeller is usually embossed on its side. The other measurement of a propeller is its diameter. This is the diameter of the circle described by the blade tips.

In practice, the choice of propeller depends on many variables that include the power from the engine, the speed of the shaft, and the speed of the propeller through the water. The type of boating that you do should also be taken into account. Dive boats are often fully laden travelling out to the dive site and then very lightly loaded while diving takes place and fully loaded again for the

Propeller pitch affects the performance of the boat

return journey. So, some compromise in choosing a propeller is inevitable. Your engine dealer should be able to help with practical advice.

In general, a coarser pitch gives a higher boat speed and works best with a lighter boat, but it may not allow the fully laden boat to climb onto the plane. A finer pitch, which gives a lower top speed, will overcome this but may allow over-revving of the engine when the boat is empty.

If your boat has the wrong propeller you may notice periods when the engine races but the propeller does not produce much thrust. These are signs of cavitation, which can occur if you have too much pitch or not enough blade area. A damaged propeller can also cavitate. When you notice the signs of cavitation you must immediately throttle back until the propeller bites again. In the long term you may see erosion of the propeller blades, called cavitation burn.

Cavitation is caused by the propeller itself. As the propeller rotates and creates thrust, the water pressure on the aft side of the blades increases and on the forward side decreases. If the pressure reduces far enough, it allows the water to boil, even at sea temperatures. Bubbles of water vapour are formed on the forward sides of the blades. These gas bubbles cause the propeller to race and the collapsing bubbles cause the erosion. If your propeller is prone to cavitation, it is not suitable for your requirements and you will need to change it.

Propeller with shear pin

Propeller with splined hub

A propeller guard can be a useful safety feature. It is a cylindrical metal guard that encases the propeller. It prevents the propeller blades from coming into contact with objects in the water: objects will bump into the guard rather than be cut by the propeller. However, propeller guards reduce the efficiency of the engine by as much as 25 per cent.

Fitting a propeller

The link between the propeller and its shaft is designed to be weak, so that if you hit an underwater obstruction it fails and any damage is limited to the fixing system and maybe the propeller. If the weak link does not fail, shock loads sent up the transmission can cause severe damage to the engine itself.

Many small engines use a simple shear pin, which fits through a hole in the propeller shaft. When the propeller is slid onto the shaft it engages with the pin and has to turn with the shaft. On impact the pin shears and the propeller spins freely. Shear pins can suffer metal fatigue, so you should carry a spare.

Larger outboards use splined hubs. The propeller centre is shaped to fit onto the longitudinal ridges of the splined drive shaft. The weak link is a rubber bush between the splined hub and the rest of the propeller. The propeller is held in place by a castellated nut and split pin.

Removing and re-fitting the propeller

Even if your propeller does not need changing it is useful to remove it and re-fit it once a year to prevent it seizing onto the shaft.

- Before working on the propeller make sure the engine is disabled by removing the ignition key and putting it in your pocket. If the engine does not have a key, disconnect the spark plug leads.
- Straighten the split pin, or tab washer, and remove it.
- Undo the propeller nut and remove it.
- Remove washers, noting their position.
- Remove the propeller, noting any further washers.
- Remove any debris or the remains of the shear pin. Debris can damage the gearbox seal.
- Coat the shaft in non-graphite grease and reassemble. Use a new shear pin if needed.
- Tighten the propeller nut according to the manufacturer's instructions. Do not over tighten.
- Re-fit a split pin or tab washer.

Fuel mixtures

The fuel tank vent, or bleed screw, must be opened to allow fuel to flow out of the tank

Fuel mixtures

The fuel tank is just a container to hold the fuel until it is needed by the engine. There are three types: portable, in-built or integral. Integral tanks are only found on smaller outboard engines. All fuel tanks need to have a vent open to the air during use, to allow fuel to be sucked out of the tank by the engine. The vent should be closed for transport or storage. A common cause of fuel starvation of the engine is to leave the tank vent closed.

In-built fuel tanks are often fitted under the deck or in the console of RIBs. However, in an inflatable it is more usual to have a portable tank. They are best stored on the deck close to the engine as this reduces the length of fuel line needed and the chances of it being snagged or cut. The ride in an inflatable can be bouncy and the fuel tank may need to be restrained, either using a strap or a tank-shaped frame that makes a recess on the floor to prevent the tank sliding around.

Any remote tank system has a rubber primer bulb to pump fuel to the engine during the starting process. When the engine is running the engine's internal fuel pump takes over. Fuel tanks may or may not have a fuel strainer built in to remove coarse debris from the fuel as it leaves the tank, but most outboards now have an in-line fuel filter fitted somewhere under the cowling. This is

easily changed if it gets clogged up, and will prevent more serious problems deeper in the engine. A common problem can be water in the fuel, so a separator should be fitted and mounted on the transom.

Two-stroke engines can run on any grade of unleaded petrol. The octane rating becomes irrelevant when oil is added to the fuel. Your manufacturer's handbook will specify the mix of oil to fuel to use in your engine. Always use good quality outboard engine 2-stroke oil, do not use standard 2-stroke oil. If your outboard is linked to an oil injection system, the oil goes into its own reservoir. Modern variable ratio oil systems automatically adjust the fuel to oil ratio to suit the engine's need as judged by the use of the throttle at the time.

Otherwise, you must add oil to each tank of fuel before use. You will need a fuel storage policy to ensure that the engine is never run on un-oiled petrol. Adding the oil as soon as you fill a tank with fuel works well, as then you know exactly how much fuel you have added to the tank and the job is done as soon as the fuel is put on board.

Four-stroke outboard engines are lubricated by a supply of oil kept within the engine in a tank or sump. User maintenance is confined to topping up and changing the oil frequently and changing the oil filter. Four-stroke engines run on unleaded petrol.

Checking the fuel supply at sea

- Is there fuel in the tank?
- Is the fuel line connected properly?
- Is the tank vent unscrewed?
- Is the fuel line trapped, cut or blocked?
- Is the fuel line cracked or perished?
- Is the in-line fuel filter blocked?
- Squeeze the primer bulb to check whether fuel is reaching the fuel filter
- If you have not yet found a problem, it could well be the carburettor, which cannot easily be fixed at sea

Checking the electrics at sea

- Check the kill switch is connected correctly
- Check all the battery connections – does the electric tilt work?
- Check under the cowl for any loose or broken wires
- Remove the plugs
- Fit the plug leads to replacement plugs and check for a spark from each by earthing each plug against a clean unpainted metal surface, holding the lead with insulated pliers, and turning the starter. Take care to earth them properly to protect the electronic ignition and do not hold any bare metal parts of the system or you will receive an electric shock
- If all plugs spark, replace them and try to start engine
- If they do not spark there is not much more you can do at sea

Fault-finding at sea

An ideal dive boat set-up would include two engines; the second to keep you out of danger or get you home if the first engine fails. This could be achieved by having a main engine and a much smaller auxiliary for emergencies, or by having twin engines running side by side all the time. If you have an auxiliary engine, remember that it should be run frequently and maintained in the same way as your main engine – after all when you need it, you really need it.

It is, however, possible to carry out some basic fault-finding at sea if you have engine trouble. A tool kit and spares pack should be kept in a waterproof container on board (see *Engine tool kit and spares*, page 70).

If your engine stops or won't start at sea, it is most likely to be due to a problem with either the fuel supply or the electrics. It may be nothing more than a loose wire or a disconnected fuel line. Also, check that you have not run out of fuel. If the engine has spluttered to a halt it is most likely to be a fuel problem. Sudden and total loss of life suggests an electrical problem.

If the engine vibrates violently or delivers erratic thrust then the propeller may have been damaged. You should stop immediately and inspect the propeller. Continuing at speed could damage the gearbox. If the boat does not move at all when put into gear, and you have a shear pin then it has probably broken. If the tiller becomes detached, you can maintain steerage by moving the whole engine by hand or by strapping an emergency tiller, such as a paddle to the engine.

Outboard maintenance

Maintenance

Your outboard engine will give you many hours of trouble-free motoring provided that you care for it. Some tasks should be carried out at least once a season (see *Periodic maintenance of all outboard engines*, page 73) and at the end of the season the engine can be put to bed for the winter if you will not be using it (see *Winterising all outboard engines*, page 73). Such periodic maintenance may be carried out by professional service engineers or by an enthusiastic owner.

Some maintenance tasks should be carried out after each boat trip. You should wash the external surfaces of the engine with fresh water after each use. Ideally the cooling system of all types of outboard engines should be flushed through after each use, particularly if you have been out in salt water. There are three ways of doing this. Small outboards can easily be run in a flushing tank, that is a container of fresh water that will take the drive leg immersed to its usual running depth. Run the engine at fast idle for a few minutes.

Flushing adaptors are available for some engines. You simply screw the adaptor into place, usually on the engine or drive leg, and attach a garden hose. Turn the water on and run the engine for a few minutes to remove all the salt.

Flush muffs are available to suit any engine whose water intakes are on the sides of the gear housing. They look like earmuffs. The cups fit over the cooling water intakes and the spigot attaches to a garden hose. As long as the muffs do not slip, you can turn the hose on and run the engine at fast idle for a few minutes.

If you have a four-stroke engine, you should check the oil level using the dipstick each day before use. It is normal for an engine to use a small amount of oil, but if you notice a sudden increase in use you should suspect a problem. If you need to top up the oil, wait a few minutes before re-testing to allow the new oil to settle.

Grease is an important lubricant of the many joints and control linkages on an outboard engine. It also protects

> ### Workshop safety
> - Wear suitable, close fitting clothing and tie back long hair, to avoid getting caught in moving machinery. Wear safety glasses
> - Never run a petrol outboard in an enclosed space, the fumes are poisonous
> - Do not smoke or use a naked flame in the vicinity of petrol, it is flammable
> - Avoid contact with petrol by wearing protective gloves, it can irritate your skin
> - Do not touch any part of the High tension (HT) circuit when the engine is turning, you may get an unpleasant electric shock or burn
> - Never run an engine without a source of cooling water, you could damage it
> - Be aware that a propeller may "creep" or spin fast enough to cause injury, even when the engine is running in neutral
> - Do not attempt to remove a propeller without disabling the engine, by removing the key or disconnecting the spark plug leads

bare metal surface from corrosion. Almost any type of grease is suitable, but never use graphite grease on any marine equipment. Graphite in contact with metal and seawater causes a chemical reaction which eats away the metal. You may need to apply grease by hand or using a grease gun. A small paintbrush can be useful for reaching inaccessible places.

You need to do more than just top up the oil

Periodic maintenance of all outboard engines

Once a season, you should have the following tasks carried out. You may need to refer to the manufacturer's instructions or use a service manual. It makes sense to do this at the beginning of the season.

• Check primer bulb and fuel hoses for deterioration.
• Remove end fittings from hoses and blow through with compressed air to remove any dirt
• Drain carburettor and flush out any accumulated sludge
• Fit a new in-line fuel filter
• Check main fuel filter and remove debris
• Replace spark plugs
• Inspect water pump impeller and replace if it shows any signs of wear
• The oil and oil filter on four-stroke engines should be changed every season or every 100 hours of use
• Gearbox oil should be checked every 3 to 4 months
• Grease the following points:
  – swivel and tilt pins
  – clamp screws
  – reverse lock
  – steering cable and joints
  – throttle cable and joints
  – gear shift mechanism, exposed parts
  – propeller shaft.
  – Never use graphite grease on any marine equipment
• Battery connections should be cleaned and protected with petroleum jelly. Unsealed batteries should have fluid levels checked and topped up. You may need to charge the battery at the start of the season
• Control cable connections should be checked for wear and tear and the exposed sections greased

Winterising all outboard engines

If your engine is going to be stored for an extended period, such as over the winter, there are certain things that should be done to reduce corrosion.

• Remove the cowl, clean the power head with a degreasing agent and wipe dry
• Remove spark plugs and introduce two or three squirts of outboard oil into each cylinder. Turn over the engine to distribute the oil on the cylinder walls. Replace old plugs
• Check for loose nuts and bolts and loose wiring. Tighten as appropriate
• Lubricate all greasing points and re-grease control cables
• Drain gearbox oil and check for signs of water. If the oil is grey and emulsified, the seals may be leaking. The engine should be checked by a professional service engineer. If there are no apparent problems, replace the oil
• For four-strokes only: change engine oil
• Replace anti-corrosion anodes if they have reduced to less than half of their original size
• Touch up any paintwork damage
• Store the engine in a dry, well-ventilated place
• Fit new spark plugs at the start of the season

Engine first aid

Saving a drowned engine

It is not that unusual to accidentally, totally immerse an outboard engine: outboards are awkward to carry and easy to drop; boats capsize. Four-stroke outboards and engines that were running when they drowned should be kept immersed, ideally in fresh water but in sea water if that is all there is, until they can be taken to a professional. Once an engine wet with salt water is exposed to the air, corrosion begins, and it progresses remarkably rapidly.

There is some simple first aid for two-strokes that have been immersed while not running. However, prompt action is essential: hours not days.

The inboard option

As RIBs used as dive boats increase in size, it is becoming more common to consider fitting a diesel inboard engine.

The greater torque generated by a diesel engine means that at lower engine speeds the engine delivers greater power than a petrol engine. So a RIB with an inboard diesel can get on the plane quicker, carry more weight, and uses less fuel. Fuel consumption can be reduced to almost a third of that of an equivalent petrol engine.

Diesel is also safer to store, as it is less flammable than petrol, because of its higher boiling point. And litre for litre, diesel is cheaper, especially when you consider that marine engines can use red diesel, which has a special low rate of duty. This reduces the fuel cost even further to around a tenth of the cost of that for a similar petrol outboard.

However, diesel inboards do take up more space in the boat than a petrol outboard and they are heavier: about one and a half times the weight of the equivalent petrol outboard.

Practical steps to save a drowned engine

- Remove cowl, spark plugs, air filter and recoil system
- Flush ignition electrics with a jet of fresh water. Squirt it through the holes in the flywheel and under its rim. Use plenty of water to remove the salt
- Separate any electrical connections and flush these too. Pay particular attention to the spark plug cap
- With the engine lying down and spark plug holes uppermost, pour water into the cylinders and turn the flywheel
- With the carburettor uppermost, pour water into the carburettor throat
- Dry the engine as best you can and spray the ignition system and electrical contacts with a water-displacing oil
- Reconnect all electrics except the stop switch and kill switch
- Refit recoil starter
- Mount engine upright and turn it over repeatedly until no water comes out of the spark plug holes
- Spray water-repellent oil through the spark plug holes into the cylinders and through the carburettor into the crankcase, turning the starter as you do so
- Clean and dry each spark plug, connect it and check for a spark by resting it on a bare metal part of the engine and pulling the starter. If there is no spark, check the connections and check that you have reconnected the stop switch or kill switch
- Remove the carburettor drain plug and pump fuel through using the rubber primer bulb or by pulling the starter. Catch any fuel that comes out. Refit the drain plug
- Clean and dry the spark plugs, refit them, attach plug leads and refit air filter
- Try to start the engine using full choke and full throttle
- It may be that more water will get into the cylinder now so remove the spark plugs and pull the starter cord a few times to expel the water
- Repeat the last three steps, until the engine starts. Run it under load for at least one hour. Use up to double the normal oil-to-fuel ratio to recoat the engine
- This engine will still need professional help

Boat trailers

Many people buy a custom-built trailer with their boat. This will have been designed to fit the boat perfectly and will no doubt satisfy any legal requirements for lighting and braking (see *Trailing and the UK law*, page 76).

A RIB requires a trailer with supports that follow the contours of the central part of the hull. This usually means a design with rollers and possibly a pivoted swing beam at the rear to help the initial moves on and off the trailer. In addition, boards on either side, or more rollers, help to stabilise the hull and minimise sideways movement.

Inflatable boats do not need the same type of support, and being lighter they may not even need rollers. More of the weight is in the side tubes, and flat boards are used, which are contoured to the shape of the hull and tubes. This makes for a light, manoeuvrable trailer. The important thing is to distribute the weight of the boat evenly on the trailer. Any undue pressure could damage the boat.

There should be enough room between the nose of the boat and the tow hitch to allow a complete reverse turn without the boat touching the side or rear of the towing vehicle. Trailer suspension must be sufficient to handle the total weight of the boat, including boat equipment, fuel and diving gear if you regularly tow with it in place. Double axle trailers are available for heavier loads. Heavier trailers may require brakes (see *Trailing and the UK law*, page 76).

The boat's transom should not overhang the trailer as the transom supports the considerable weight of the engine. There should be enough room for the engine, set on tilt, between the back of the trailer and the light board. If the boat is towed with the engine in the normal 'down' position there is a risk that the skeg and gearbox will be damaged by contact with the ground. Engines should be towed on full tilt and locked into position. To avoid problems if the tilt mechanism fails during a journey, a support such as a block of wood can be tied into place between the engine leg and the boat transom. This will hold the engine up if the tilt mechanism fails.

Some trailers are designed to have their wheels submerged to launch and recover the boat. Specially designed wheel hubs keep the wheel bearings sealed from the water. Unprotected wheel bearings require frequent re-greasing as salt water replaces the grease and corrosion rapidly occurs. Once you have submerged the trailer you should re-grease the bearings – certainly, this should be done before any significant amount of towing on the road. Wheel bearings heat up during use and some greases become more liquid when heated and do not necessarily remain in place. So, it is vital to use the correct type of grease, which depends on how you use your trailer. If you tow long distances on the road, you should use grease suitable for bearings in constant use. If you merely push your trailer to and from the water's edge, you could use specialist waterproof grease designed for boat trailers.

Choosing a boat trailer

When choosing a trailer for a boat, the following factors have to be taken into consideration

- Type of boat
- Size of boat
- Weight of boat
- Size and weight of towing vehicle
- Type of launch – dry or wet
- Amount and type of road use

Engines and trailers **75**

Loading your trailer

Loading your trailer

Many of the problems associated with towing a trailer are caused by incorrect loading. Here are some tips:

- Put all heavy items over the axle and make sure they are secured to prevent movement when cornering or braking.
- Put heavier items in the car and larger lighter items in the trailer.
- Consult your trailer and vehicle handbooks to establish the correct nose weight for your trailer. For most cars it is 50kg to 100kg.
- To check your nose weight, place a flat piece of wood on your bathroom scales (to spread the load and prevent damage to the scales). Lower the jockey wheel of the trailer onto the centre of the wood and adjust the angle of the trailer so that it is level.
- To be more accurate, put an upright length of wood between the coupling head and the flat piece of wood on your scales, ensuring the trailer is level.
- Check the weight shown on the scales and compare with your car/trailer requirements
- If incorrect, adjust the trailer load to compensate.
- Finally, check the load is secure and cannot move. It is always good policy to recheck your load after a few miles to confirm everything is secured properly.

Trailer maintenance

At the beginning of the season your boat trailer should be thoroughly checked over. Wire-brush the metal and check all welded joints for cracks. Check all rollers and boards and replace if necessary. Check the fixing straps for wear and tear, replace if they become frayed. Check the tyres for wear. Check wheel bearings, brakes and brake cables for wear and lubricate them. If brake cables and linkages seize then the brakes may bind, causing the wheel bearings to overheat. This could result in the wheel, complete with hub, falling off the trailer.

Wheel bearings are the most vulnerable part of the trailer, being subject to both wear and tear on the road and the corrosive effects of seawater during launching and recovery of the boat. It is important to keep them well greased at all times. If the trailer is simply used to move the boat in and out of the water, at a boat park for example, there are special waterproof greases designed for boat trailers. Otherwise, grease suitable for road use should be chosen. It will be designed to stay in place as the bearings heat up in use.

You will need to take a correctly inflated spare wheel, plus the tools needed to change it, on every trip that you make. It makes sense to carry a spare set of wheel bearings as well.

Trailing and the UK law

When you add a trailer to the back of your car, it inevitably has a very serious effect on the vehicle's performance. Starting your vehicle, particularly on hills, will be more difficult. Stopping will take a much longer time and you will travel a longer distance. Cornering and negotiating sharp bends will require extra care.

Vehicle manufacturers quote a maximum trailer weight for any vehicle. If this is exceeded it is possible that the courts or insurance companies may take the view that this constitutes a danger. Remember that this weight must include the boat itself and any items in it or on it. The police use the manufacturer's recommended towing limit as their guide to determine whether you are safe.

There are various other rules set by government agencies that you must obey when towing a trailer on the road. The weight of an un-braked trailer is limited to half of the kerb weight of the vehicle, or 750 kg, whichever is less. The weight of larger braked trailers should not exceed 85 per cent of the kerb weight of the vehicle.

A trailer with a maximum laden weight of more than 750 kg must be braked. You must also have a braked trailer if the laden weight of the trailer exceeds half of the weight of the towing vehicle.

Trailer board components are specified by law

If the gross weight of the towing vehicle is 3.5 tonnes or less, the maximum permissible width and length of a trailer are 2.3 metres and 7 metres respectively. A boat is permitted to overhang the width of its trailer to a total width of 2.9m. Nearly all vehicles used to tow small dive boats will fit into this weight limit.

For trailers weighing up to 1,500 kg when laden, you must have a secondary coupling that will, in the event of separation of the main coupling, retain the trailer attached to the towing vehicle, prevent the nose touching the ground, and provide some residual steering of the trailer. This can be a wire strop on the trailer tow hitch attached to a U-bolt on the car's tow ball plate.

Any load overhanging the rear of a trailer by between 1 and 2 metres must be clearly marked when towing. A good solution is to tie a stout bag in a visible colour over the propeller.

Trailers must have on the back: two red sidelights; two red stop lamps; an illuminated number plate; two triangular red reflectors; and amber indicators that flash between 60 and 120 times per minute. If the trailer is more than 1.3 metres wide, it must also have at least one red fog lamp. If there is only one, it must be fitted to the offside or on the centre line of the trailer. All trailers built after 30 September 1990 require front reflectors. Boat trailers do not require front-position lamps.

Car and trailer tyres must have at least 1.6mm of tread over the central 75 per cent of their width for their entire circumference, although a tyre with under 3mm offers little grip in the wet. Tyres must be free from deep cuts and bulges (which indicate they are breaking up) and it is illegal to use cross-ply and radial tyres on the same axle. Make sure that the tyres you fit to your trailer are of the correct rating.

As stated in *The Highway Code*, cars towing trailers must obey the following speed limits: 30 miles per hour in built-up areas; 50 mph on single-carriageway roads; and 60 mph on dual carriageways. Vehicles towing trailers are not allowed in the outside lane of a three-lane highway.

All trailers must be fitted with an approved-style number plate. A trailer marking plate should be fitted to the nearside of the trailer drawbar. It should show the manufacturer's name, serial number, number of axles, maximum weight for each axle, maximum load imposed on the drawing vehicle, maximum gross weight and year of manufacture of the trailer.

The Highway Code rules for vehicle towing

- You must not tow more than your licence permits
- You must not overload your vehicle or trailer
- You must secure your load and it must not stick out dangerously
- You should properly distribute the weight in your trailer. Heavy items should be over the axle and there should be a downwards force on the tow-ball. Manufacturer's recommended weight and tow-ball load should not be exceeded. This should avoid the possibility of swerving and going out of control. If this does happen, ease off the accelerator and reduce speed gently to regain control.

Requirements

Driving licensing requirements for towing trailers in Great Britain

- You must hold a full driving licence to tow anything.

- Most drivers who passed a driving test before 1 January 1997 are entitled to drive a vehicle and trailer combination weighing up to 8.25 tonnes maximum authorised mass (MAM), that is combined gross weight. This should include most club boat set-ups.

- The Second European Commission Directive on Driving Licences (91/439/EEC), which came into effect on 1 January 1997, states that drivers who passed their test on or after that date can only drive a B category vehicle (MAM less than 3500 kg and not more than eight passenger seats). They are not allowed to tow a trailer and are required to take another test with a towing trailer. When the driver has passed their test the MAM of the trailer is 750Kg laden weight. For divers some club boat set-ups may not fall into the scope of the licence held by the driver and may require an additional driving test.

- Further details from: Driver and Vehicle Licensing Agency, National Trailer and Towing Association Ltd, motoring organisations such as the RAC and AA.

Information to give your boat insurer

When you are setting up insurance for your boat you will need to have the following information. Policy details may vary between insurers, so it is worth spending some time finding the best policy for you.

- Value, model and serial number of boat, including maximum designed speed

- Value, model and serial number of outboard engine(s)

- Where you routinely store your boat when it is not in use

- Details of fixings used to secure the engine(s) to the boat

- Details of how you immobilise your trailer

- Inventory of boat kit that you expect to be covered, including electronics

- Inventory of personal effects

- Details of any safety equipment required by the insurer, such as fire extinguishers

- Type of boating use

- Specific details of any permanent mooring used

Insurance

Vehicle insurance is compulsory: to drive on the road you must have an insurance policy. When you are driving you could injure someone or cause damage to someone's property, and the law states that you must be able to compensate the other person. The law can be sure you will be able to do this by making you take out insurance.

The minimum type of insurance the law requires is called third party only. While this is cheapest, most people will want to add fire and theft cover because it only costs a little more. Many people prefer comprehensive policies because they also cover damage to your own vehicle.

From a boat owner's point of view, your vehicle policy will also insure you against an accident involving any trailer that is attached to your car, at the level you have chosen. So, for example, a third party only car insurance package will cover any liability you may have to someone else because of an accident involving a trailer, but it will not compensate you in any way. Also, you will only be covered for vehicles and trailers that you are licensed to drive and tow (see *Trailing and the UK law*, page 76).

You must bear in mind that, at all levels, your vehicle insurer will not be liable in respect of any claim arising out of damage to, or loss of, the towed trailer or any property being carried in it or on it. In other words loss or damage to the trailer, the boat and its contents will not be covered.

There is no requirement to insure your boat before you drive it at sea. But it is sensible to consider your liabilities. For example, what would happen if someone was injured while using your boat? Specific insurance policies are available for sports boats. They will cover loss or damage to the vessel and its trailer, including theft, during transport on the road and during use at sea. They can also provide third-party liability cover.

Insurers usually specify that the trailer should be securely immobilised – you can do this with a wheel clamp, or by storing in a secure building when it is left unattended. They also require that outboard engines are secured to the boat with anti-theft devices, in addition to the normal fixings. These should be some type of lockable fixings. Damage to tyres is not usually covered. Damage to personal kit is not usually covered, although you may well be able to make provision for that.

Policies may include special clauses for speedboats, which could be defined as boats that have a maximum designed speed of as low as 'more than 17 knots'. This would include most branch dive boats. Restrictions put on such boats could include safety requirements such as having a fire extinguisher on board. They could also impose mooring restrictions, such as not leaving the vessel afloat and unmanned off any shore, unless the mooring has been approved by the insurer. This last requirement could mean that your dive boat is not insured if you leave it moored.

There will probably be an excess applied to accidents where you damage the boat by hitting a submerged object. As with any type of insurance, it is vital to check the detail of your policy. The cheapest may not be the most suitable for you. Specialist insurance brokers are the best source of current advice.

Chapter four

Safety at sea

Parts of the International Convention for the Safety of Life at Sea – otherwise known as SOLAS – directly affect all pleasure boat users. Most of the convention only applies to large, commercial ships, but parts of Chapter V apply to all vessels on all voyages, including small, privately owned pleasure craft. This will include all club or individually owned dive boats, as well as charter boats.

If you are involved in a boating accident and it is shown that you have not applied the basic principles of SOLAS V, you could be prosecuted.

There are five areas of advice in SOLAS V that should be taken into account each time you go to sea.

- Voyage planning
- Radar reflectors
- Life-saving signals
- Assistance to other craft
- Misuse of distress signals

In addition to SOLAS V, pleasure boats users are bound by the International Regulations for the Prevention of Collisions at Sea (IRPCS or COLREGS), the International Convention for the Prevention of Pollution from Ships (MARPOL) and vessels more than 13.7 metres in length are required to meet certain life-saving and fire-protection requirements.

The rules of the road

When driving a car, you are expected to follow certain rules - *The Highway Code* - to ensure the safety of others. Not surprisingly there are also rules of the road at sea. They are contained in the International Regulations for Preventing Collisions at Sea 1972 (IRPCS). This set of 38 rules applies to all vessels at sea and they are fundamental to safety at sea. Let us take a look at the most important rules for small vessels.

The skipper of any vessel has certain general responsibilities. A proper look out, by sight and sound, must be kept at all times and in all weathers (rule 5). Vessels are required to proceed at a safe speed so that they can take action to avoid a potential collision (rule 6). It is every vessel's responsibility to determine when there is a risk of collision (rule 7) and to take action to avoid collisions (rule 8).

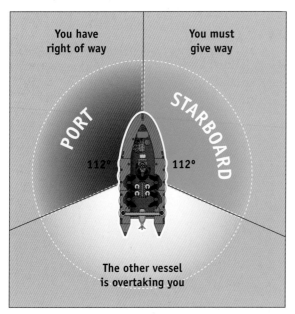

The correct action to avoid collision depends on which sector an approaching vessel is in

Narrow channels

If you are driving in a narrow channel you must keep as far to the starboard side of the channel as possible (rule 9). It is best to avoid crossing a traffic lane or other channel in which large vessels are restricted to a well-defined route. They are unlikely to alter course if you get in their way, so if you have to cross, try to do so at right angles to the traffic and keep well clear at all times (rule 10).

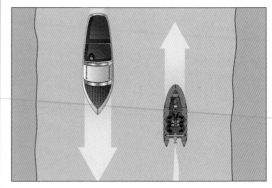

Keep to starboard side in a narrow channel and pass port to port

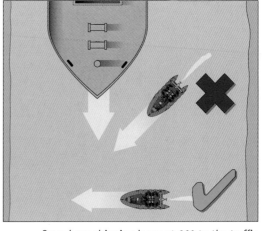

Cross busy shipping lanes at 90° to the traffic

Overtaking

When overtaking another vessel you must keep well clear and allow it plenty of sea room (rule 13). Inflatables and RIBs are highly manoeuvrable and should easily be able to keep clear of other craft.

Keep well clear when overtaking

Meeting head-to-head

When meeting another vessel head-on, you should turn to starboard, as should the other vessel (rule 14). The vessels should end up passing port side to port side.

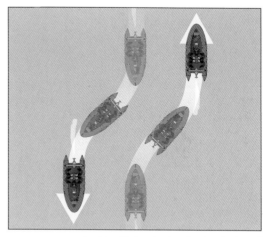

Avoid collision by turning to starboard

Right of way

If a vessel is approaching from your starboard side and there is a risk of collision, you must give way (rule 15). You should slow down and allow the vessel to cross your path or bring your vessel around behind the other. Any action should be taken early and it should be clear to the other vessel that you are taking avoiding action. Inflatables and RIBs are highly manoeuvrable and should easily be able to keep clear of other craft.

Give way to a vessel on your starboard bow

Power gives way to sail

Collision avoidance

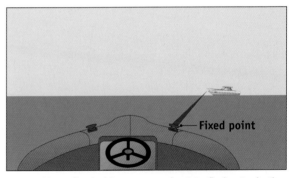

To find out whether you are on a collision course with another vessel, stay still in your boat and pick an object on your boat that lines up with the other vessel. Watch for a while and see whether the other vessel appears to move relative to the object you have chosen. If the other vessel appears to move backwards you are moving faster and if you both maintain current speed and direction you will pass in front of the other vessel. If the other vessel appears to move forwards, you will pass behind it. But if the other vessel appears to stand still you are on a collision course and action must be taken.

Use a fixed object on your boat to find out whether you are on a collision course with another vessel. If there is no change in your relative position, you are on a collision course.

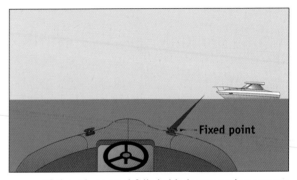

Responsibilities between vessels (rule 18)
A power-driven vessel shall keep out of the way of:
- A vessel not under command, unable to manoeuvre through exceptional circumstances
- A vessel restricted in ability to manoeuvre
- A vessel engaged in fishing
- A sailing vessel.

If the other vessel falls behind your marker, you are going to pass in front of it

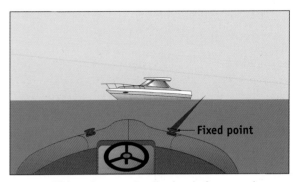

If the other vessel pulls ahead of your marker, you are going to pass behind it

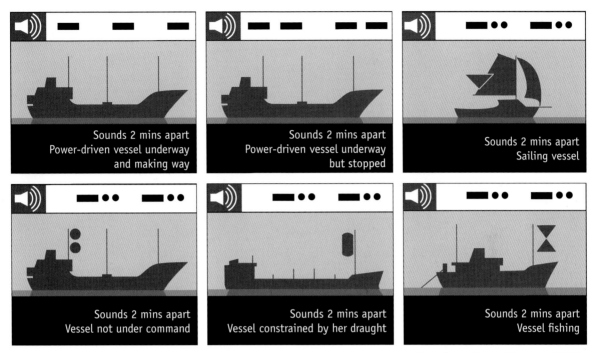

Sound signals used in poor visibility

The rules of the road, discussed here, govern how any two vessels should interact in most situations encountered at sea, but if the other vessel is much larger than you it makes a difference in practice. Large vessels, moving at top speed, take a long time to change course or slow down: they may not be able to take avoiding action in time to prevent a collision. In such situations, it is necessary for those in a small boat to take avoiding action even if they have right of way. Also large vessels have difficulty seeing small vessels in front of their bows; even if you have right of way it would be more sensible for the small boat to take any action needed.

Detailed extracts from the International Regulations for the Prevention of Collisions at Sea are given in the *Appendix* on page 168 of this manual.

Dive boats may encounter situations where the surface visibility becomes restricted – such as fog, sea mist, heavy rain or indeed nightfall. In such conditions sound becomes more important than sight. In restricted visibility, if you hear a fog signal coming from forwards of your beam you are required to reduce speed to the minimum to keep you on course until the danger of collision is passed (rule 19). Vessels of less than 12 metres in length are not obliged to use the regulation sound signals to warn others of their presence in conditions of restricted visibility, but they must make some other efficient sound signal at intervals of not more than 2 minutes (rule 35).

Lights

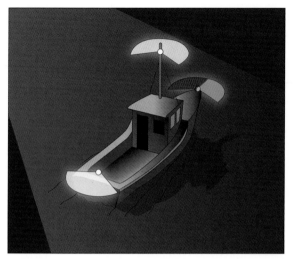

Positions of lights on a vessel

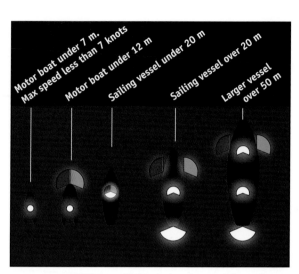

Lights to be shown while underway at night

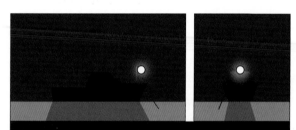

Power-driven vessel under 7 m (Lights not required if not in channel, fairway or anchorage)

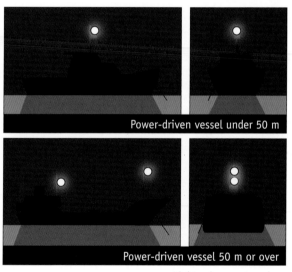

Power-driven vessel under 50 m

Power-driven vessel 50 m or over

Lights shown at anchor

It is also useful to be able to tell what a particular vessel is doing at any time, as this will affect how you manoeuvre around it. At night, vessels display additional lights for this purpose. During the day, lights are difficult to see and there is a system of shape signals. Technical specifications for lights and shapes can be found in Annex I of the international regulations. The light and shape signals are given in part C of the IRPCS (for details see *Appendix*, page 168). Vessels less than 12 metres in length do not have to display the shape signals except if they are engaged in diving operations, when they must display a rigid replica of the international code flag 'A' that is not less than 1 metre in height (rule 27).

Signals to be used by vessels in distress are given in Annex IV of the IRPCS. We will discuss them and their uses in the section of this book about emergencies at sea (see *Chapter V*, page 94).

As well as the rules contained within the IRPCS, boat users actions can be governed by harbour and local byelaws. These particularly relate to local speed limits and areas of restricted use, for example swimming-only areas at beaches. Always ask the harbour master about any local restrictions.

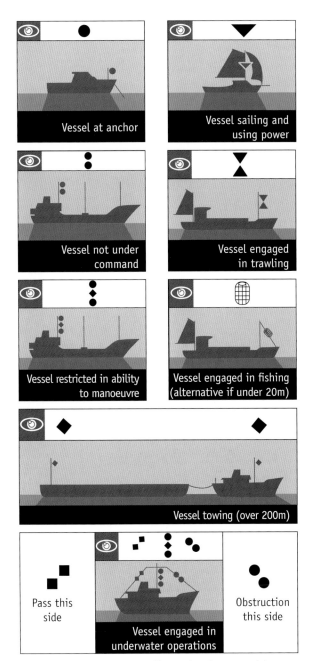

Shape signals are used to warn
other vessels

Buoyage

The sea, by its very nature, has fewer recognisable features to navigate by than the land. Also underwater features can have a big impact on shipping, but are largely invisible to the mariner. So various systems of signs to mark safe waters and dangers have been used at sea.

Today the International Association of Lighthouse Authorities' Maritime Buoyage System helps mariners of all nationalities to navigate at sea and avoid dangers. The IALA system is mainly designed for commercial shipping, but it can provide divers with valuable information to help with position fixing, wreck location and pilotage. The system provides rules to mark the lateral limits of navigable channels, natural and other dangers to shipping, and other areas or features of importance.

For the purposes of the system, the countries of the world are divided into two buoyage regions. Region B comprises the Americas, Japan, Korea and the Philippines. Region A comprises the rest of the world.

Within the system there are five types of marks, which may be used in combination: lateral marks; cardinal marks; isolated danger marks; safe-water marks; and new danger marks. The lateral marks differ between buoyage regions A and B. All other marks are the same worldwide.

Marks may be displayed on moored, floating buoys, or on permanent structures in shallow water, such as beacon towers, breakwaters or even simple painted wooden poles. The distinguishing characteristics of the different marks are their shape, top mark, colour, and at night the colour and rhythm of their lights.

Lateral marks

Lateral marks

These are generally used to define the port and starboard sides of a navigable channel. Their purpose is to show the mariner the general direction to take when approaching a harbour or waterway from seaward.

This can only be done if a direction of travel is agreed on. This 'conventional direction of buoyage' is shown on appropriate nautical documents, such as charts. In a straightforward situation, such as a vessel approaching or leaving a harbour or other waterway, the buoyage is set up as if the vessel is approaching from seaward.

In practice then, when approaching a harbour from seaward you should keep a port hand mark to port and a starboard hand mark to starboard. When leaving this will be reversed: the port hand mark will be passed to starboard and the starboard hand mark passed to port.

In places less well defined by features on land the direction is fixed by the authorities and, in principal, follows a clockwise direction around land masses. In the UK the conventional direction of buoyage follows the main flood tide from the south-west tip of the country northwards up both east and west coasts.

Lateral marks are the only marks that differ between IALA regions A and B. In IALA region A, the port hand mark is a red can, pillar or spar with a red light. The starboard hand mark is a green cone, pillar or spar with a green light. In IALA region B the shapes remain the same but the colours are reversed. So port hand marks are green cans and starboard hand marks are red cones.

Cardinal marks

Cardinal marks are pillar or spar-shaped buoys coloured yellow and black. Distinctive colour patterns and double cone top marks are used to distinguish between the four cardinal marks; north, south, east and west (see diagram, right).

They are used in conjunction with a compass to show that the deepest water in an area lies to the named side of the mark, and that is the safe side on which to pass the danger. A north cardinal mark, for example, indicates that deep water is to be found to the north of the buoy.

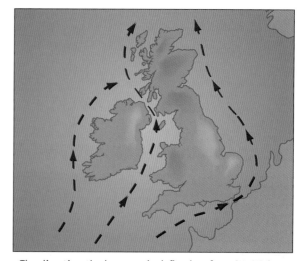

The direction the buoyage is defined as from SW-NE in UK waters except when approaching harbours and estuaries

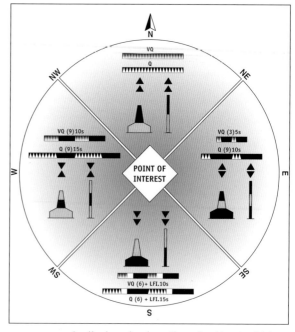

Cardinal marks show the safe side on which to pass a danger

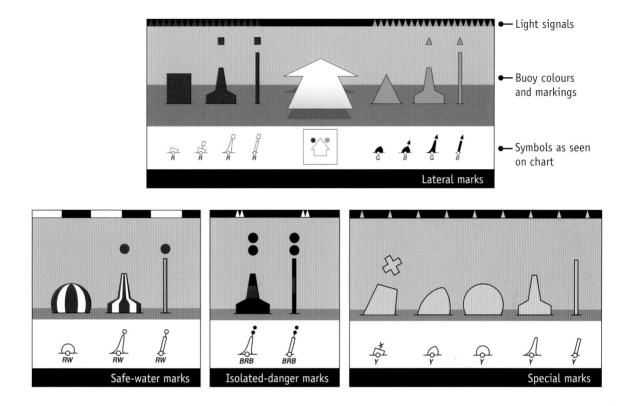

Light signals — Buoy colours and markings — Symbols as seen on chart — Lateral marks — Safe-water marks — Isolated-danger marks — Special marks

Safe-water marks

These spherical, pillar or spar-shaped buoys, with red-and-white vertical stripes, have navigable water all around. They have a single red spherical top mark.

Isolated-danger marks

These are placed on small dangers with navigable water surrounding them. They are black pillars or spars with at least one broad horizontal red band and a top mark of two black spheres, one above the other.

Special marks

Special marks are not intended for navigation, instead they show you where certain types of features, marked on a chart, actually are. They may mark spoil grounds, military exercise zones, recreation zones and so on. They are yellow marks with a yellow X-shaped top mark.

New-danger marks

Recent hazards, which do not appear on charts yet, are marked as soon as possible by duplicate sets of the appropriate marks until they are charted.

The typical dive boat has a relatively shallow draught; in the case of a RIB it may need only 1 metre of water below the keel. This means that RIBs can drive over most of the sea and so it seems that there is little use in learning about buoyage systems, but the knowledge gained will help you to predict what other shipping will do around you. Also by looking at a chart you can now find buoys to use for pilotage. Today we rely heavily on onboard electronics for position fixing, but it is always worthwhile having another plan to get home in case of electrical failure.

Features that are hazardous to dive boats, such as barely submerged rocks, are often very close to shore and are almost always unmarked as commercial shipping does not pass that close to land. Such dangers must be identified from a chart or other source of local knowledge.

Radios and communication

Radios and communication

Good communication between the boat and the shore is an invaluable part of any dive boat set-up. At the very least you must be able to send a message of distress in an emergency using an internationally recognised distress signal or a flare. It is even better if you can get up to date weather and safety information while you are at sea, and exchange details of an emergency with the rescue services. Very High Frequency, or VHF, radio is an affordable way of communicating ship-to-ship or ship-to-shore with a range of up to 60 nautical miles for large vessels. It is unlikely that you will find other types of radio on small dive boats.

Cellular phones may seem to offer low a cost alternative to marine VHF. However, if you are in distress they have several significant weaknesses.

- Cellular networks offer poor coverage at sea.
- You can only ring one number, for example the coastguard, so other vessels close by will be unaware of your situation and therefore unable to offer assistance.
- If you are on the fringe of a cell, you can very easily lose contact.
- Lifeboats and helicopters are not equipped to obtain a bearing on phone signals.

Routine use of VHF radio

You are strongly advised to carry a marine VHF radio on board your diving boat. As a bare minimum the set should be able to transmit and receive on channel 16, channel 6 and at least one other channel. Its output power should be suitable for the distances over which the boat operates. Portable or hand-held radios may be limited to an output of 5 watts. These are best suited for use over short distances because of their small aerials and limited power. To be able to transmit and receive signals from more than 15 miles offshore you will require a set

The range of VHF radio communication

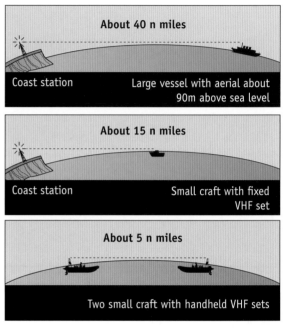

The higher the aerial the farther a VHF signal can travel

with a maximum output of 25 watts.

The range of your VHF radio depends on the height of both transmitting and receiving aerials as well as the power output of the radio set. It is essentially line of sight or slightly better. Local weather conditions can have an affect on the transmission range, usually to decrease it.

If your eye, or aerial, is 2 metres above the sea's surface, you will be able to 'see' an object on the horizon 2.9 nautical miles away. If you raise the height of the transmitting and receiving aerials you will increase the range of communication between the two. Tables giving the distance away of the horizon for various heights are included in nautical almanacs.

There are three modes of operation of VHF sets. Simplex sets transmit and receive on the same frequency, meaning that only one person can speak at any time. Semi-duplex sets transmit and receive on different frequencies, but still only one at a time. And duplex sets use two different frequencies simultaneously to allow normal conversation.

How to use a typical VHF radio

1 Switch set on and set volume control to midway

2 Select channel

3 Adjust squelch control until background noise is barely audible

4 Use low power. If there is no response to repeated calls change to high power. Be aware that unecessary use of high power can block other calls to the receiving station. This is to be avoided.

5 Hold microphone 5cm from your mouth

6 Press the switch to transmit (press-to-talk or PTT switch) and speak normally

7 Release the switch immediately after speaking and await a reply

Describing your position at sea

Before making radio calls you need to understand the standard ways that position is described at sea (position fixing is described in more detail in *Chartwork*, page 115).

- **Position** is either given as true position in degrees, minutes and seconds, latitude followed by longitude or as a distance and compass bearing **from** an object eg. *"I am 2 miles from the Eddystone lighthouse, bearing 315°"*
- **Course** in degrees from true north
- **Bearings** from true north, given either from the mark or the vessel
- **Relative bearings** could be expressed in degrees relative to a vessel's bow
- **Distance** in nautical miles or kilometres
- **Time** in the 24-hour clock
- **Speed** in knots, that is nautical miles per hour, through the water
- If you need to name features, use the names given on the chart

The frequencies used to send and receive signals are known by their international channel number, and are grouped for three main purposes: public correspondence; inter-ship communications; and port operations (see *Proper use of VHF channels at sea*, page 92).

All use of maritime radio transmission equipment is covered by one of two types of UK licence. A Ship Radio Licence gives you a unique call sign and allows you to set up an account to use paid-for telephone services through coast stations. A Ship Portable Radio licence covers the use of portable radios not covered by a ship licence. You need one of these if, for example, you want to use a hand-held radio on more than one vessel or if you want to use a 406 megahertz or a 121.5 MHz personal locator beacon or emergency position indicating beacon (EPIRB see *Radio beacons*, page 104).

In addition, there is an international requirement for anyone sending a transmission to either have a recognised operator's certificate or be closely supervised by someone who has. Operator's qualifications are designed to ensure that users understand the correct procedures for all situations. The most common certificate in the UK is the Short Range Certificate, which covers routine, safety, urgency, and distress communications using VHF/digital selective calling equipment.

There are some rules governing general calls made on VHF radio. You should use the correct maritime radio procedure for establishing contact. First listen to check that your chosen channel is free of traffic. Then press and hold the PTT button and, slowly and distinctly, call a station three times and give your callsign (or your vessel type and name) three times. For example: 'Falmouth coastguard, Falmouth coastguard, Falmouth coastguard, this is dive boat Alpha, Alpha, Alpha'. Do not interrupt transmissions already in progress – wait for an appropriate break before starting your call. Give way if asked to do so by a coast station.

If a station does not reply to a call sent three times at two-minute intervals, stop calling. Resume at three-minute intervals at the earliest, having made sure that the station is not talking to someone else. Take the least time that you can to establish contact on channel 16, one minute should be the maximum, then, switch to another inter-ship channel.

How to use a VHF radio

Proper use of VHF channels at sea

- Marine VHF radios and any operators must be licensed. Other persons may get the permission of the operator to use the equipment under supervision.

- All signals must be preceded by your identification, for example the vessel's name or callsign or maritime mobile service identification number (MMSI).

- Channel 16 may only be used for distress, urgency and very brief safety communications, or for calling to establish other communications, which should be then concluded on a suitable working channel.

- Channels 6, 8, 72 and 77 are available in the UK for routine ship-to-ship communications.

- Channel 13 is designated worldwide as a navigation safety communication channel. It is used for bridge-to-bridge voice communications under the GMDSS, and is monitored by commercial vessels if there is a danger of collision.

- Channels 10, 67 and 73 are set aside internationally for coordinated search and rescue operations. Channel 10 can also be used in reporting pollution. Channels 67 and 73 are also coastguard working frequencies.

- Certain channels are locally set aside for port operations, they should not be used for other purposes.

- Channel 70 may only be used for digital selective calling (DSC, see The GMDSS, page 96).

- If your vessel does not have DSC, you should maintain a listening watch on channel 16.

The phonetic alphabet

Voice technique is important when transmitting on the radio. A slightly higher pitch than normal will sound clearer. Hold the microphone a few centimetres away from your mouth and speak at normal volume. You will need to speak slowly and clearly. Use the phonetic alphabet wherever possible. The alphabet is used with the following English pronunciations.

The following pronunciation is used for numerals. All numbers are transmitted by saying each digit separately, except that whole numbers of thousands are transmitted as the digit(s) followed by the word thousand. For example 12,000 would be 'one, two, thousand'.

Letter	Word	Pronunciation
A	Alpha	al fah
B	Bravo	brah voh
C	Charlie	char lee
D	Delta	dell tah
E	Echo	eckk oh
F	Foxtrot	foks trot
G	Golf	golf
H	Hotel	hoh tel
I	India	in dee ah
J	Juliet	jew lee ett
K	Kilo	key loh
L	Lima	lee mah
M	Mike	mike
N	November	no vem ber
O	Oscar	oss cah
P	Papa	pah pah
Q	Quebec	keh beck
R	Romeo	row me oh
S	Sierra	see air rah
T	Tango	tang go
U	Uniform	you nee form
V	Victor	vik tah
W	Whisky	wiss key
X	X-ray	ecks ray
Y	Yankee	yang key
Z	Zulu	zoo loo

Number	Pronunciation
0	zee ro
1	wun
2	too
3	tree
4	fower
5	fife
6	six
7	sev en
8	ait
9	nine er
decimal	day se mal
thousand	tousand

Chapter five

Emergencies at sea

Successful boating depends on many things: equipment, weather, and people – to name just a few. Whenever you take to sea, there is a chance that something will go wrong and you should be prepared. Some emergencies you will be able to deal with yourself. Others may escalate and put lives at risk. It is important to know what the emergency services can offer and when to call them in.

If you are in such a small craft one of your basic, never to be missed, safety procedures should be to telephone the coastguard before leaving for a dive, with an outline of your activities and a promise to call back when you return safely to shore. An alternative is to have a reliable shore party ready to raise the alarm if you are well overdue. In these situations, it is important to stick to your original plan and it is important to make that return call.

Most diving takes place around the coastal areas of the world where there is usually good emergency backup, such as from the coastguard services. Diving in more remote places where such backup is not available requires extra equipment and extra expertise.

When distress occurs at sea, the situation is affected by how well the divers and crew react, and how well equipped the boat is. Here we discuss the safety regulations that apply to small pleasure boats and what to do if a serious incident occurs.

Distress at sea usually involves either accident, illness or injury to people or some kind of equipment failure, usually involving the boat or engine. For medical reasons, it may be necessary to evacuate a casualty. If equipment fails, the boat, divers and crew may need rescuing. You and your divers and crew need to be prepared to deal with the following emergencies: overdue divers; medical emergencies; man overboard; capsize; boat adrift; damage to a boat; towing another boat; and fire.

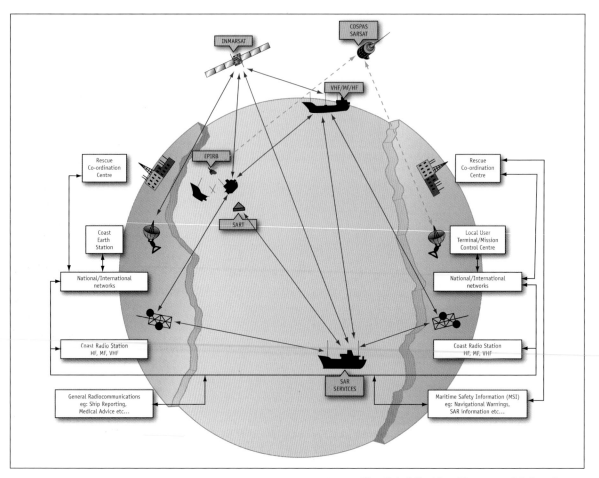

The Global Maritime Distress and Safety System

The Global Maritime Distress and Safety System

Chapter IV of the International Safety of Life at Sea convention (SOLAS) set out the biggest change to maritime communications for commercial shipping since the invention of radio: the Global Maritime Distress and Safety System. The GMDSS, which came into force in 1999, affects more than just voice communication at sea, although one of its most obvious effects is to introduce a digital system to VHF radio called digital selective calling.

The basic concept of GMDSS is that search and rescue authorities ashore, as well as shipping in the immediate vicinity of a ship in distress, will be rapidly alerted to a distress incident, without maintaining a listening watch on radio, so that they can assist in a co-ordinated search and rescue operation with the minimum delay. The system also provides for communication of navigational and meteorological warnings and forecasts, and other urgent safety information to ships.

GMDSS consists of several different safety systems based around different communication technologies. These include digital selective calling for VHF radio, Navtex weather and navigation information, search and rescue radar transponders (SARTs) and emergency position indicating radio beacons (EPIRBs). Under the GMDSS, all distress and safety communication will be automated – keeping watch on traditional voice and Morse code frequencies will become history.

At the press of a button, a ship can send its identity, position and the nature of its distress by either satellite or terrestrial radio communication. It will then be up to a shore-based Rescue Coordination Centre (RCC) to alert vessels in the area to go to the aid of the stricken vessel. This coordinating role of the RCC is a new one. Previously, ships were required to monitor for distress alerts and then respond directly. The GMDSS now makes this the responsibility of the coordination centre.

The use of GMDSS for small pleasure craft is voluntary, but the UK coastguard strongly recommends that such vessels have Digital Selective Radios: DSC is a fundamental part of GMDSS. All small-craft fixed VHF radios now on the market are GMDSS-compatible – but to benefit from GMDSS you may have to buy the DSC element separately. All UK coastguard stations are GMDSS/DSC equipped.

Digital selective calling is simply a tone signalling system, which operates on VHF channel 70 and is similar to tone dialling on land-based telephone networks. It has the ability to include extra information such as the vessel's identification number, the purpose of your call, your position, and the channel you want to speak on, all sent as bursts of digital code. With the present VHF system you have to listen to all calls to determine which are for you; with DSC, an alert rings on your vessel when there is a call for you.

Already, shipping does not have to maintain a listening watch on channel 16, though many vessels still do and the UK coastguard has stopped its dedicated headset listening on channel 16. A loudspeaker watch will continue at each coastguard station, but this will rely on someone in a busy control room hearing a distress call against a background of other noise.

On a DSC set, a distress call giving the precise position of your boat can be sent by simply pushing a button if connected to a GPS set. It will be heard immediately by all DSC equipped vessels and shore stations, and will be automatically repeated every four minutes until it is acknowledged, either by a coastguard station or a ship within range. Any DSC distress alerts should be followed up with a voice distress call. Safety information broadcasts will generate an alert, ensuring that you do not miss them. Routine calls to others also become easier: you just have to enter their dedicated number, select a working channel and send the call. Both radios will be set to the chosen channel automatically for the conversation.

When you first license a radio, or at any subsequent time, you can request a nine-digit Maritime Mobile Service Identification number (MMSI) which is your unique electronic call sign and is essential to operate DSC.

For other important ways that SOLAS affects pleasure boats see *Safety at Sea*, page 80.

Responsibilities of the skipper

Responsibilities of the skipper

The skipper of a vessel is responsible for the safety of the vessel and all those aboard. The skipper also has certain responsibilities to aid any other vessel in distress at sea. The following parts of Chapter V of the International Convention for the Safety of Life at Sea (SOLAS) describe the responsibilities of the skipper and they apply to all vessels on all voyages at sea.

You are required to respond to any distress signal that you see or hear, and help anyone or any boat in distress as best you can (regulations V/31, V/32 and V/33). You must also let the coastguard and any other vessels in the vicinity know if you encounter anything that could cause a serious hazard to navigation, if it has not already been reported. You can do this by calling the coastguard on VHF or by telephoning them at the earliest opportunity. The coastguard will then warn other vessels in the area.

Regulation V/35 prohibits the misuse of any distress signals. These are critical to safety at sea and by misusing them you could put your own, or someone else's life at risk.

Regulation V/29 details the signals that ships, aircraft or persons in distress should use to communicate with the search and rescue services or other boats when you are in trouble. You are required to study the signals before you go boating and, if practicable, to carry a copy of the table of signals on board.

Distress signals

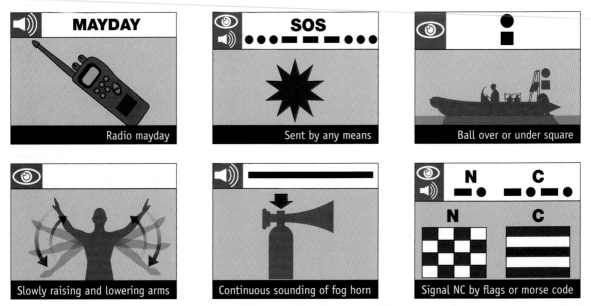

The internationally accepted distress signals for use at sea are described fully in Annex IV of the IRPCS (see *Appendix* page 168)

Distress calls on VHF radio

If a vessel or person is in grave and imminent danger and help is urgently required, you will need to use channel 16 to transmit a mayday call. A distress call has priority over all other transmissions. It is useful for all divers and crew to know how to send a distress message. The mayday message format should be on display close to the radio, along with the life saving signals required by SOLAS.

Once your distress message has been completed, release the PTT button and listen. In coastal waters, you should get an immediate acknowledgement. It will take the form of: 'Mayday (your name, spoken three times), this is (name of station acknowledging, spoken three times), received mayday'. If you do not get an acknowledgement, check your set and repeat your distress message.

If you hear a distress call, cease all transmissions that might interfere with it and listen on the frequency concerned. If you can help, you should acknowledge the call, but only once you have given the nearest coastguard station or some larger vessel the chance to do so.

If you hear a distress call that is not acknowledged you should try to pass it on. This is done using a mayday relay message. On channel 16 say the following: 'Mayday relay, mayday relay, mayday relay, this is (your callsign/vessel name, repeated three times)'. Then repeat the intercepted message.

Although mayday calls impose a general silence on the radio until the call is cancelled, a station controlling distress traffic may want to impose further radio silence. To do this they will say: 'Seelonce mayday, (controlling station's name)'. Radio silence can be relaxed by the controlling station using the signal 'prudonce' in this way: 'Mayday, all stations, all stations, all stations, this is (controlling station name), (the time), (the name of the vessel in distress), prudonce'. In the same way, radio silence can be cancelled using the signal 'seelonce feenee'.

An 'urgency' message can be sent if you have a very urgent message about the safety of a ship or person. You use the urgency signal 'pan-pan'. Messages prefixed by pan-pan take precedence over all others except distress

---

Emergency calls on radio

There are three types of emergency signals on marine VHF radio: distress, urgency, and safety calls

- A distress signal is sent when there is grave and imminent danger to a vessel or person and immediate assistance is required. Use the distress signal 'mayday'.

- An urgency message is sent when you are in a situation that involves the safety of a boat or person, but it will not launch all the rescue services at that moment. Use the urgency signal 'pan pan'.

- A safety signal is the least serious degree of emergency, usually associated with a warning of navigational or meteorological hazard. Use the safety signal 'securité'.

Making a 'mayday' call

- "Mayday, mayday, mayday"
- "This is RIB Dive, Dive, Dive."
- "My position is..."
- (State nature of distress)
- "Assitance required..."
- (State number of people on board)
- "Mayday RIB Dive, over".

---

calls, and are sent on channel 16. The urgency signal could be used if you have lost divers or if you need urgent medical advice, for example in a case of decompression sickness. Here is an example of an urgency call: 'Pan-pan, pan-pan, pan-pan, all stations, all stations, all stations, this is dive boat (your name or callsign, repeated three times)'. Followed by a brief description of the problem and the help that you require. You must end with, 'over'. You will probably be directed to a working channel and the coastguard will ask for more detail about the case, before deciding what action to take.

'Safety' signals are prefixed by the word 'securité', repeated three times, and they indicate an important navigational or meteorological warning.

DSC procedures

DSC procedures

• Calling another ship

– If you know the Maritime Mobile Service Identification number (MMSI) of the other vessel, enter it into the controller and select which working channel you wish to use. When the called set rings you should start the call as follows: 'Station calling (vessel name), this is (vessel name), over'.

– If you do not know the MMSI of the other vessel, call using ordinary VHF procedure on channel 16. If no response, call again on channel 13, which has been allocated for bridge-to-bridge communication in GMDSS

• Sending a distress call

– Send a distress alert using DSC, by pressing the alert button. Wait about 15 seconds for acknowledgement from the coastguard or a ship station.

– Then, on channel 16, transmit your distress call in the normal way giving the nature of your distress, the assistance required, the number on board and any other relevant information. If your radio is linked to GPS DSC the coastguard will already know your position.

– If no acknowledgement is received, but an offer of help is accepted from another vessel cancel the alert.

• Acknowledging a distress call

– A distress alert will cause any DSC controller to sound an audible alarm. You should cease all transmission that may interfere with distress traffic and listen on channel 16. Coast stations and some other vessels are capable of responding to a DSC alert using DSC. If there is no such acknowledgement, after a short interval you should acknowledge the call by voice, using normal VHF procedure on channel 16.

• 'All ships' alerts

– A vessel outside of coastal station range, can issue a safety warning using the all ships safety facility. After about 15 seconds, the safety call and message will be transmitted by voice on channel 16, using normal VHF procedure and the prefix securité.

• Calling coast stations

– Enter the MMSI of the coast station into the controller. When you get acknowledgement the responder will indicate a working channel and the DSC set will retune automatically and as the caller you should initiate the call on this channel.

SAFETY INFORMATION

VHF Radio – Channel 16 or DSC
MAYDAY / PAN PAN

CALLING _____ (COASTGUARD)

THIS IS: _____ (BOAT IDENTITY)

I HAVE A DIVING/BOAT EMERGENCY AT:

_____ (POSITION)

I REQUIRE ASSISTANCE/CASUALTY EVACUATION TO

_____

I REQUIRE AN AMBULANCE AT: _____

MY ETA IS: _____

MY VESSEL IS A: _____

THE PARTY CONSISTS OF _____ PERSONS

Ashore – at coast, ring 999 – ask for Coastguard.

Ashore – inland, ring 07831-151523 state that you are dealing with a diving emergency and ask to be put through to the RN Superintendent of Diving if you are calling in business hours. At other times ask to be put through to the Duty Diving Medical Officer.

In Scotland call 01224 681818 (Aberdeen Royal Infirmary)

SUSPECTED DECOMPRESSION ILLNESS/BAROTRAUMA	FIRST AID
Seek expert advice Give 100% oxygen as soon as possible – continuously. Lie casualty down.	Maintain breathing/circulation Remove from danger Stem bleeding Treat shock Seek help

Distress flares

In the event of an emergency, flares are one of the most effective means of attracting attention. They must be in good condition, in date and have clear instructions for their safe operation. Flares suitable for use in small boats usually have a shelf life of three years, so when you buy them check the expiry dates and replace them accordingly.

There are four types of flare that are useful for vessels sailing in inshore waters, up to 3 miles from land, or coastal waters, 3 to 15 miles from land: red parachute; red hand-held; orange smoke and white hand-held flares.

Red parachute rocket flares can be seen for up to 28 miles on a clear night. They are used to send a distress signal and mark your position when you are out of sight of land. The flare hangs burning in the air for more than 40 seconds from a small parachute. The higher up it goes the better it will be seen, from a distance. So you must consider getting the flare in the right place. They should be fired almost vertically if there is no wind. In windy conditions, fire them 15 degrees downwind – the rocket will curve gently into the wind by design. In low cloud, fire them at 45 degrees downwind – so that the flare deploys below 1,000 feet.

Red hand-held flares can be visible for up to 7 miles on a clear night. They are used to send a distress signal in inshore waters, and are useful to pinpoint your exact position when rescuers are in sight. They should be used when you are in sight of the shore or other vessels. They are powerful pyrotechnic devices and should always be fired with an outstretched arm, pointing downwind and away from the boat.

Orange smoke flares are used to send a distress signal and pinpoint your position in daylight, when they are more effective than flares, especially in bright conditions. They can be seen for up to 3 miles, although the smoke disperses in windy conditions.

All flares should be fired downwind, pointing away from the person and the boat. There is no point in firing them if there is no one around to see them. For the same reason, never fire all of your flares at once. In the first instance, let off two flares within two minutes. Keep one red hand-held flare for night use and one orange smoke flare for daytime use in reserve. Never use parachute flares when helicopters are operating nearby and only use hand-held flares to pinpoint your position when requested to do so by the search-and-rescue team. Hand-held flares used at night will disrupt your night vision – shield your eyes from the flare.

In reply to your flare, you should see either an orange smoke signal, or three white star rockets fired at intervals of about one minute. These signals mean: 'You are seen – assistance will be given as soon as possible'.

The other type of flare that you may see fired is the white hand-held flare, which is used to warn another vessel of an impending collision. They are essential for making night passages.

All flares should be kept in a waterproof container, kept somewhere readily accessible. All divers and crew should know how to fire them. In an inflatable or RIB it is best to have a separate, waterproof emergency box for flares, diver recall signals and other emergency kit (see *What should an emergency box contain?* page 104). This box should not be opened routinely. It should, however be checked at regular intervals.

Distress flares

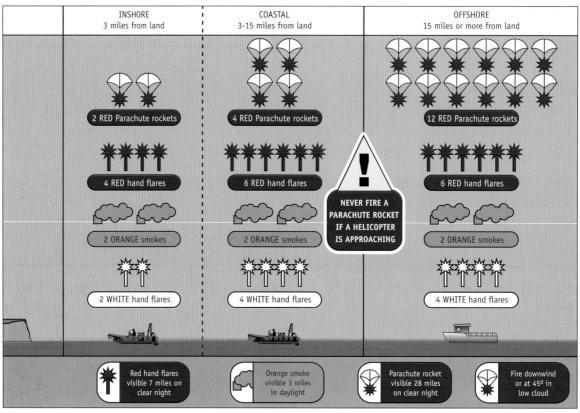

	INSHORE 3 miles from land	COASTAL 3-15 miles from land	OFFSHORE 15 miles or more from land
	2 RED Parachute rockets	4 RED Parachute rockets	12 RED Parachute rockets
	4 RED hand flares	6 RED hand flares	6 RED hand flares
	2 ORANGE smokes	2 ORANGE smokes	2 ORANGE smokes
	2 WHITE hand flares	4 WHITE hand flares	4 WHITE hand flares

NEVER FIRE A PARACHUTE ROCKET IF A HELICOPTER IS APPROACHING

Red hand flares visible 7 miles on clear night

Orange smoke visible 3 miles in daylight

Parachute rocket visible 28 miles on clear night

Fire downwind or at 45° in low cloud

Types of distress flares

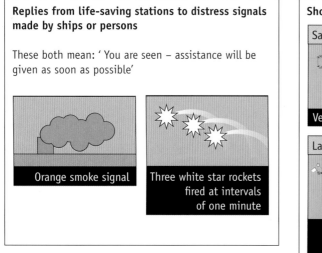

Replies from life-saving stations to distress signals made by ships or persons

These both mean: 'You are seen – assistance will be given as soon as possible'

Orange smoke signal

Three white star rockets fired at intervals of one minute

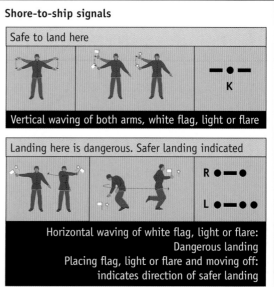

Shore-to-ship signals

Safe to land here

Vertical waving of both arms, white flag, light or flare

— • —
K

Landing here is dangerous. Safer landing indicated

R • — —
L • — • •

Horizontal waving of white flag, light or flare:
Dangerous landing
Placing flag, light or flare and moving off:
indicates direction of safer landing

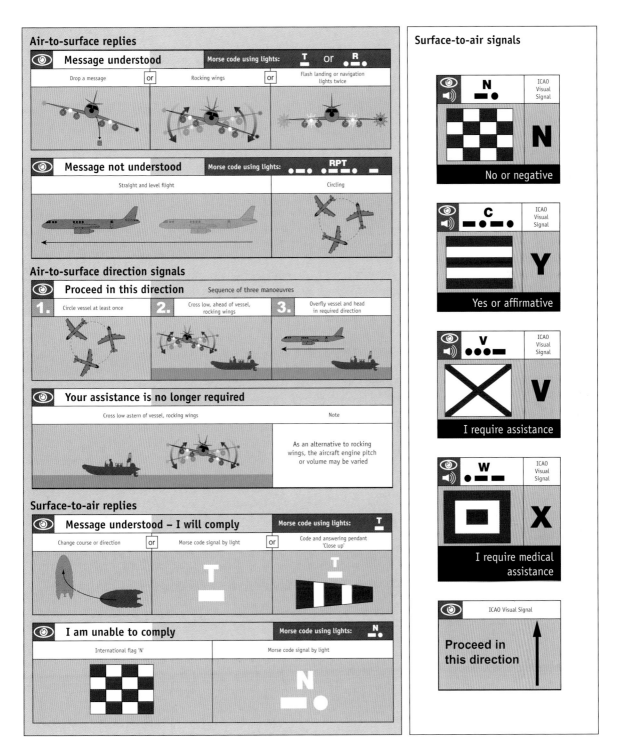

Air-to-surface replies

Message understood
Morse code using lights: **T** or **R**

Drop a message   or   Rocking wings   or   Flash landing or navigation lights twice

Message not understood
Morse code using lights: **RPT**

Straight and level flight   Circling

Air-to-surface direction signals

Proceed in this direction
Sequence of three manoeuvres

1. Circle vessel at least once
2. Cross low, ahead of vessel, rocking wings
3. Overfly vessel and head in required direction

Your assistance is no longer required

Cross low astern of vessel, rocking wings

Note

As an alternative to rocking wings, the aircraft engine pitch or volume may be varied

Surface-to-air replies

Message understood – I will comply
Morse code using lights: **T**

Change course or direction   or   Morse code signal by light   or   Code and answering pendant 'Close up'

I am unable to comply
Morse code using lights: **N**

International flag 'N'   Morse code signal by light

Surface-to-air signals

N — ICAO Visual Signal

No or negative

C — ICAO Visual Signal

Yes or affirmative

V — ICAO Visual Signal

I require assistance

W — ICAO Visual Signal

I require medical assistance

ICAO Visual Signal

Proceed in this direction

Emergency box

What should an emergency box contain?
- Flare pack, differs depending on your expected distance from land (see below)
- 6 diver recall signals
- Exposure blanket
- First aid kit containing wound dressings, triangular bandages, safety pins (for details see *First aid kits*, page 101)
- Torch and batteries

Flare packs
Inshore waters – up to 3 miles
- 2 x red rocket parachute flares
- 4 x red hand-held flares
- 2 x orange hand-held smoke flares
- 2 x white hand-held flares

Coastal waters – 3 to 15 miles
- 4 x red rocket parachute flares
- 6 x red hand-held flares
- 2 x orange smoke floats
- 4 x white hand-held flares

Offshore waters – in excess of 15 miles
At distances in excess of 15 miles the use of flares is very limited as a means of attracting attention. Flares should only be used if another vessel or aircraft can be seen and is heading towards your position. More reliance should be put on the DSC/VHF radio, GMDSS equipment or an EPIRB to identify your position and distress situation. However, the following flares are recommended.

- 12 x red rocket parachute flares
- 6 x red hand-held flares
- 2 x orange smoke floats
- 4 x white hand-held flares

Diver recall signals

You should consider how to provide a suitable means of recalling your divers should the need arise. Whatever method is used divers must be clearly briefed on what to expect and what action to take when such a signal is deployed.

Giving four strong pulls on the line of a surface marker buoy is a recognised diver recall signal. It is, however, possible to confuse rope signals on an SMB line with the tugs generated by the surface movement of the buoy, so if there is no response, you can increase the number of tugs. It is also possible to slide a negatively buoyant plastic disc attached to the SMB line down to the diver, or to drop a strobe down the SMB line.

If no other method is available, you could use your engine to make a signal. Go near to the divers' position and rev your dive boat engine repeatedly, in neutral. However, your divers might simply interpret this to mean that their cover boat is getting impatient.

Thunderflashes are manufactured specifically as a pyrotechnic diver recall signal. In an emergency, you follow the instructions to light the thunderflash and release it into water near to but not directly over your divers. A loud underwater bang alerts the divers and tells them to surface. The thunderflash must be weighted to be negatively buoyant. Divers should be able to experience a thunderflash going off, as a training drill, so that they will recognise it when they experience it in a real situation. Six thunderflashes should be added to your emergency boat box.

Radio beacons

An Emergency Position-Indicating Radio Beacon, or EPIRB, is a small, self-contained, battery-operated radio transmitter designed to facilitate search and rescue operations. It is buoyant and watertight, and can be designed to activate automatically when immersed in water. Once immersed, the EPIRB emits a signal that is picked up

EPIRBs are activated by immersion in water

by dedicated satellites or local search and rescue services. There are several different types of EPIRB, transmitting on different frequencies, and suited to different uses. Sometimes they are called personal locator beacons. EPIRBs are designed to supplement a vessel's VHF radio communications – they should not be fitted instead of a VHF radio.

EPIRB transmissions on 406 megahertz send a digital signal to the COSPAS/SARSAT system of polar-orbiting satellites, which are a part of the GMDSS (see *The Global Maritime Distress Safety System*, page 96). The information is then downloaded to local user terminals across the globe and passed to the national search-and-rescue service, who can obtain positional information and vessel details for use in any rescue plan. Positional accuracy is initially 2 to 4 miles, and this improves with additional satellite passes.

EPIRB transmissions on 121.5 MHz are used only for precise direction finding purposes by SAR services once a rescue has commenced. Units that transmit on 121.5 MHz only are not useful as a means of alerting the rescue services.

Commercial vessels may be required to have a 406/121.5 MHz, 48-hour duration EPIRB with a hydrostatic release mechanism mounted on their superstructure. The hydrostatic mechanism has a life of 2 years and must be in date. It automatically ejects the beacon if submerged in a few metres of water. The EPIRB floats free of the vessel and begins to transmit. Smaller vessels may choose a manual release, 406/121.5 MHz unit with an active duration of 24 or 48 hours. These can be stowed near to the navigation station, for use in an emergency. They have to be removed from their canister and placed in the water.

Manual or water-activated distress beacons transmitting only on 121.5 MHz, with a power output of 75 milliwatts and a duration of 24 hours are useful as a radio direction beacon to enable SAR services to get a radio position fix on you during a search. These can be mounted on a vessel's bulkhead or worn on the body. Some can be programmed with your radio call sign or your unique DSC identity

(MMRI). You should check the specification of such devices carefully as some use interrupted and not continuous transmission, for example. Manual or automatic personal locator beacons with only a 25 mW power output, usually worn on the body, have a very limited use as short range, man overboard locators.

All EPIRBs have a unique identity, which is programmed into them during manufacture. It is important to register your EPIRB with the relevant authority, in the UK that is the MCA, in order to link your vessel's details with the beacon.

EPIRBs should be stowed somewhere readily seen and available for use. They should not be allowed to move freely or be stored near devices with magnetic properties, which could cause them to accidentally activate. For transport to repair or servicing outlets, EPIRBs should be completely wrapped in two layers of aluminium foil. This will provide suitable radio frequency screening.

The authorities spend a great deal of time and money chasing up accidentally activated EPIRBs. If you accidentally activate one you should radio or telephone the coastguard immediately to cancel the alert. If you activate an EPIRB during an episode of distress at sea, however, you should not switch it off until the incident is over.

An EPIRB is a radio transmitter and so it must be added to your radio licence. If you already have a callsign, then your ship radio licence can be updated to include the EPIRB. Otherwise you will need a portable maritime radio licence, which covers hand-held VHF radios and EPIRBs.

Overdue divers

Emergency situations

The responsibilities of a dive marshal include carrying out a risk assessment of any boating elements of the dive plan, but as dive boat coxswain you should also participate in that process. There are certain 'What if...' scenarios that you need to consider. The successful outcome of any emergency situation depends on how the people involved react to the emergency and it is helpful to have thought about the following scenarios before they happen to you. Then you can carry out a rescue as quickly and efficiently as possible.

Overdue divers

If divers have not surfaced according to plan and you suspect that they are in difficulty, you should contact the coastguard as soon as possible to discuss your concerns. However, do not stop looking out for your missing divers. Part of the responsibility of the coxswain or skipper is to be aware of local conditions affecting the dive site, such as tides and weather, and this knowledge helps you to search logically for the divers. But you should investigate anything unusual that you see in the vicinity of the dive site. Expect the unexpected. Remember to inform the coastguard if you find the missing divers first.

The coastguard can be contacted on VHF channel 16 or DSC channel 70, 24 hours a day. You will need to make a mayday or pan-pan call (see *Distress calls*, page 99). It is important to be able to state your position as accurately as possible, as well as the nature of the distress and any other information that might help. Once you have stated your position you must attempt to maintain it unless you are given other instructions.

Another way to contact the rescue services is to use your flares. Or you may be able to use one of the other internationally recognised distress signals.

You should contact the coastguard early on in any emergency. They will offer assistance throughout. Do not delay, early contact with the coastguard will give them extra time to help you and, if it turns out that their help is not needed, there will be no recriminations, just thanks all round. On the other hand, delay in contacting the coastguard could limit their ability to help.

Medical emergencies

Perhaps the most common distress at sea involving divers is decompression sickness. Depending on the severity of the symptoms, the diver may need to be taken back to base and kept under observation or may require fast, efficient transport to the nearest recompression chamber.

With a serious case, the worst thing to do may be to rush back to shore in a small boat on a bumpy sea. In the UK we have access to excellent emergency services, coordinated by the coastguard. They can organise helicopter transfers, access to a recompression chamber, ambulance, lifeboat, police escorts and they are trained to deal with all manner of emergencies at sea.

You may also have to deal with other medical emergencies, either diving-related or not, and the coastguard can get expert advice to you by radio.

First aid for diving-related medical emergencies

Following a diving-related injury, the administration of oxygen is an important first-aid measure. Oxygen should be administered as early as possible and should be administered continuously until the casualty is handed over to specialist medical care.

A suitable oxygen kit comprises of the following:

- Standard medical oxygen cylinder, size D or E
- Oxygen regulator incorporating a cylinder pressure gauge and providing an outlet for at least one demand unit, and an outlet capable of delivering oxygen at a minimum of 10 litres per minute
- Demand unit, hose and oro-nasal mask
- Pocket mask incorporating an oxygen connection elbow and a suitable hose for the delivery of oxygen at a constant flow of 10 litres per minute

Some demand units incorporate a positive pressure ventilation facility. If so, this should be limited to a flow rate of 40 litres per minute and should also incorporate an overpressure relief valve, which limits the airway overpressure to a maximum of 45 centimetres of water. In demand mode, the unit should be able to deliver a maximum demanded flow rate in excess of 100 litres per minute.

The amount of oxygen carried by a boat must reflect the normal operating range of the boat and be sufficient to avoid running out before handing a casualty into the care of the emergency services.

The administration of still fluids is believed to be beneficial in the first aid treatment of decompression sickness. A minimum of two litres of still fluid should be carried to enable you to give at least one litre per hour. When diving in more remote areas, additional fluids should be carried.

Conventional first aid is also needed to treat medical emergencies and all small boats should be equipped with an appropriate first-aid kit.

First-aid kits

This kit should provide the first-aider with the basics to attend a casualty. Its contents depend on your operating distance from medical resources ashore and the risks that the boat occupants are likely to face. The following kits are the minimum recommended in the Combined Diving Association's Guidelines for the safe operation of member club dive boats.

Small boat kit (for inshore use – up to 3 miles)

2 x large sterile dressings
1 x large pack of assorted adhesive dressings
2 x large triangular bandages
1 x rescue blanket or large polythene bag
6 x safety pins
disposable gloves

These items should be individually wrapped and sealed in plastic bags and the whole kit should be housed in a waterproof container.

Offshore kit (for use in excess of 3 miles from shore)

1 x first-aid instruction booklet
6 x each: small, medium and large standard dressings
1 x large pack of assorted adhesive dressings
4 x large triangular bandages
10 x assorted safety pins
3 x 50mm roller bandages
1 x 50mm crepe bandage
1 x roll 25mm zinc oxide plaster
1 x set of scissors
1 x set of tweezers
1 x pack of sterile cotton wool
2 x pairs of disposable gloves
1 x rescue blanket or large polythene bag
disposable gloves
pocket mask, or suitable barrier, for use when giving artificial ventilation

These items should be individually wrapped and sealed in plastic bags and the whole kit should be housed in a sturdy weatherproof container.

Additional items may be necessary if diving is to take place in more remote locations where medical resources are not readily available and the expedition is of a longer duration. In this case you should also consider the need for qualified first aid and medical personnel.

Man overboard

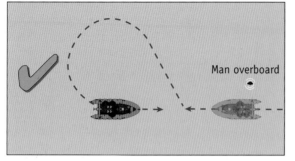

The Williamson turn places you on the reciprocal of your original course

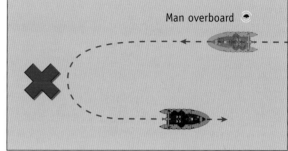

An immediate 180° turn does not place you on a reciprocal heading

Man overboard

The coxswain of a diving boat should be skilled at manoeuvring the boat when people are in the water, after all dropping off and picking up divers is, for them, a routine operation. When there is an unexpected man overboard these same skills come into play.

If anyone sees someone fall overboard they should shout 'Man overboard to port/starboard'. The first thing a coxswain should do is to make sure not to lose sight of the person overboard. It is easy to lose sight of a head in the sea even in moderate conditions. Ask someone to keep pointing at the man overboard. Also, pressing the man overboard button on a GPS unit will instantly mark your position.

If you are travelling at slow speed, make a turn to whichever side the person fell from. This will ensure that the propeller is kept away from the person in the water. Before you turn, you should inform the divers and crew so that they can hold on to the boat. To recover a conscious person, adopt the same approach as for picking up divers, using the wind and tide to your advantage.

It may be easier to lose sight of a man overboard from a bigger boat, such as a dive charter vessel. Although you have a better vantage point from a higher deck, it may be that you do not notice the incident until some time later as you are not all in such close proximity all of the time. If some distance has been travelled it is useful to return on a reciprocal (opposite) course, not a parallel one. Carrying out a Williamson turn achieves this. The vessel is turned to 60 degrees from her original heading and continues in

a straight line until there is enough room to turn onto the reciprocal of the original course. The man overboard should now be directly ahead. If he is not in sight, a search pattern should be instigated. Informing the coastguard is a sensible precaution as help may be necessary.

Getting an unconscious casualty back into a boat is difficult. You will need help in the water – a diver kitted in basics would be ideal. In a RIB or inflatable, two people can probably pull a casualty into the boat. On hard boats, because of the higher freeboard, bringing an unconscious casualty on board is harder. You could use the diving ladder to support the casualty, which would give the rescuers a rigid object to lift. Or a loop of rope passed around the upper torso and under the armpits of the casualty, tied with a bowline, can sometimes be used as a sling to help with a lift.

If a diver falls into the water wearing a wetsuit or drysuit, they will probably have enough buoyancy to float – but if they are unconscious they may end up face down in the water. Suits should not be relied upon to provide suitable flotation in the event of falling overboard and it is highly recommended that a lifejacket is worn in addition to a closed dry suit, especially for long sea trips. A suit's buoyancy is only provided if the suit's zip has been completely closed, so it is essential that all drysuit zips are closed completely and checked by a buddy before leaving shore. However a properly designed life jacket should help to turn, and keep, a person head up in the water.

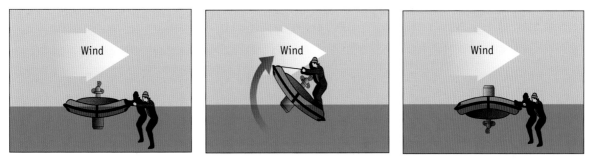

Wind and your body weight can be used to right a small capsized boat

It is recommended that all people travelling in a small dive boat, such as a RIB or inflatable, should wear a lifejacket.

Any lifejacket must provide the user with an oral inflation system, and sufficient buoyancy to support the person on the surface, with their face clear of the water. Lifejackets of an appropriate size should be made available for any passengers including children. The boat's coxswain should always wear a lifejacket.

Ideally there should always be at least two crew in a small boat, then if one should fall overboard the other can recover that person. If you are boat-handling alone, you should always use a kill switch system that uses a lanyard to connect you to the engine's short circuit switch. Then, if you move too far from the controls you will turn off the engine. This at least will prevent the boat disappearing over the horizon if you fall overboard. If you cannot find a person who has fallen overboard you should send a radio urgency call, using the prefix pan-pan, to get help from the coastguard (see *Distress calls*, page 99).

Capsized boat

A small craft can be capsized by careless handling, or swamped and rolled over by a heavy sea. If this happens to you, the immediate priority is to count heads and make sure that no one is left underneath the boat. It is best to stay with the boat, unless you are in breaking waves where the boat poses a danger to you. One reason for this is that the boat is bigger than you and easier for the rescue services to spot. It also acts as a focal point to keep the group together.

You may be able to right a small inflatable boat with a small engine and at least get the crew out of the water onto a stable platform. You should attempt this as soon as possible. Manoeuvre the overturned boat across the wind. Fix the free end of the painter to a handle or handline on the windward side. Get the divers and crew to climb on to the downwind tube and pull on the rope. The boat should start to roll towards them and the wind will get underneath and help.

This is not a practical technique for rigid-hulled boats because of their much greater weights. Dories, depending on their construction, should float when capsized, particularly if air has been trapped in the upturned boat. A capsized RIB, with undamaged tubes, will stay afloat because of the buoyancy of its tubes.

The crew and divers should stay as close as possible to an upturned boat and use the emergency flares, which should be in a box attached to the boat by a line long enough for the box to float free in the event of a capsize. It is wise to be familiar with the firing mechanisms of your flares and they should always be in date.

How close you stay to an upturned boat must be considered carefully. The boat presents a large target for the rescue services to locate but there may be loose lines floating around you, which could be hazardous, particularly if the boat is unstable and sinks. If the boat sinks the group should still stay together.

Boat adrift

Boat adrift

A drifting boat is at the mercy of the elements – wind and tide can carry it quickly into danger. Every effort must be made to stop the boat. Unless the boat is being taken towards safe water, the first thing to do is to anchor. If the water is too deep for you to anchor securely, a sea anchor can be used to slow down your drift due to the wind. Once your position is secure then you can attempt to get the engine working (see *Outboard engines, Fault finding at sea*, page 71), use alternative propulsion such as paddles, or call for help using the radio or one of the internationally accepted distress signals (see *Distress signals*, page 99).

It is essential to remain with your boat, while it remains afloat. The survival time for an unprotected swimmer in temperate regions is measured in hours. Divers may well be better kitted out, but do not underestimate how difficult it is to swim against wind and tide on the surface. Stay with the boat until help arrives.

Towing a disabled boat

Most of the boat-related incidents reported in the annual BSAC *Diving Incidents Report* are related to engine failure. Trying to repair an engine at sea is not easy. So, if you come across a stranded boat, it is useful to know how to help by towing it to safety.

To tow another powerboat of similar size any distance at sea the long tow is best. If the area around the boat to be towed is safe, approach on the leeward side and attach a rope as near to the bows of the disabled boat as you can, you could use their painter, for example. A better solution, to keep the towed boat in a suitable attitude in the water and to distribute the load evenly over the towed vessel's structure is to use a towing bridle. The bridle should be tailor-made for the boat: it should extend the length of the boat, pass through the life-lines and attach to strong points on the transom. It should be stowed in an accessible compartment and be used exclusively for towing.

Sea anchors

A sea anchor is traditionally a canvas-covered frame, an Admiralty cone or windsock type, that provides resistance when dragged through the sea. Modern sea anchors are nylon parachute types. A minimum of 10 boat lengths of nylon line is used to attach the sea anchor to the boat. Its stretch helps to absorb the load. When a sea anchor is deployed, the boat's rudder should be fixed amidships. Offshore mariners regularly use sea anchors to provide stability, for example in rough weather or to hove to for repairs. For divers, who mainly undertake short inshore voyages, they have fewer uses and can be smaller and less technical.

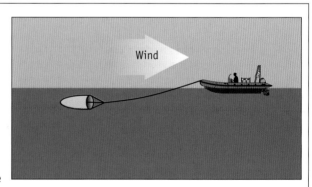

Uses of sea anchors

- To slow down a drifting boat (small drogue is sufficient)
- Towed astern to prevent broaching when running with the sea (small drogue is sufficient)
- Towed from the bows of a boat without power to keep bows into the waves (small drogue is sufficient)
- Towed astern of a boat under tow, in a following sea to increase tension on the towing line (small drogue is sufficient)

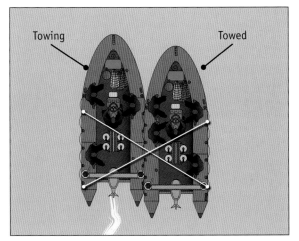

The use of springs allows the towed and towing vessel to move as one

If the disabled boat is near a significant danger, such as rocks or a lee shore, you should anchor seaward of them and then you can pay out your anchor line and drop back onto them to attach a line. Once you are attached you can pull up on your anchor to move out of danger and then move off under power. You need to fix the towrope to your transom, not to your engine. Some kind of quick-release fixing would be best. The length of the rope should allow both boats to be on the crests, or troughs, of successive waves.

Before moving off, agree to any signals to be used. Also, ask the crew to steer the towed vessel to follow the towing vessel, if they have any steerage. In a following sea the towed boat will tend to surge forward. Using a sea anchor behind the towed boat will help keep tension on the line. A sea anchor could be improvised using an anchor basket with a rope bridle, for example.

Attaching a weight, a diving weight belt could be used, midway along the towing line will help to keep the towing line under tension and prevent it fouling the propeller of the towing boat.

As you prepare to start the tow, take up the slack slowly and try to avoid snatching. The crew of the towed boat should sit as far back as possible to un-weight the bow.

The long tow, however, is not very suitable for manoeuvring close to a berth. A side tow allows two boats to operate as one. You need to attach the two boats

Salvage rights

If a vessel is not in danger, but needs assistance it is appropriate for the assisting vessel to consider whether they have a salvage claim against the rescued vessel. This can be a substantial part of the value of the rescued boat, as decided by the courts. Although in the UK this situation will not arise when the assistance is from the rescue services, such as the Royal National Lifeboat Institution (RNLI).

There are some things that you can do to avoid a salvage claim being made against you
- You should make it clear to your rescuers that you are not in danger and that you are in control of the situation, but that you need some assistance.
- You should negotiate a fee, for example for a tow to port, before any rescue is attempted. Get your divers and crew to witness any agreement. If no fee is required, a goodwill gesture from you such as offering to pay for any fuel used and making a donation to the local RNLI would be acceptable.
- You should ALWAYS pass your line to the rescuing boat. If you accept their line you will be deemed not to be in control and they will have a right to salvage.
- If you are in distress, all this is irrelevant as your rescue is paramount.
- Your boat insurance may well cover salvage claims against you – check the small print. Insurers will need to be informed of all the facts as soon as possible. Remember, if you are under-insured, your insurer may not pay the full sum awarded to the salvager.

together using crossed springs. One goes from the bow of the towing boat to the stern of the disabled boat. The other goes from the bow of the disabled boat to the stern of the towing boat. The nose of the disabled boat should be held slightly nose in, using lines from bow to bow and stern to stern. These allow you to move as one, both forward and in reverse. Ideally, any points of contact should be protected by fenders. Outboards should be lifted to reduce drag. The side tow may take a while to set up, but the mobility gained will be worth it.

Boat damage

Boat damage

If an inflatable boat becomes damaged at sea, it may be possible to carry out a temporary repair. Small punctures of the tubes can be patched with a repair kit. Larger holes and tears that could be repaired on land can be difficult to fix at sea. However, inflatables are designed with several separate buoyancy compartments and it is possible to get under way in an inflatable with a deflated compartment by holding up the fabric of the tube to form the missing side of the boat. Passing a paddle handle through the handlines of a deflated section for instance, would give good support to the fabric. It is unlikely that you will be able to move very fast and you will need to bail water out from the boat all the time.

If the tubes of a RIB are damaged, this will have most of an impact when you are stationary or travelling slowly. When a RIB is planing, the tubes are clear of the water and the rigid hull is giving the boat its buoyancy. When at rest, however, a RIB rests low in the water supported by the tubes.

The tubes are usually divided into compartments, in the same way as in inflatable boats. So it is most likely that you will only lose one compartment. If you have the time it is possible to mend a puncture at sea.

If you cannot mend the puncture, you will need to tie up the deflated section so that the fabric acts as a wall to prevent water coming into the boat. Again, it may help to thread a paddle through the hand lines of the deflated section to give the fabric some rigidity. You will be able to use grab handles on the other tube, the console, the A-frame or bottle rack as securing points.

If you damage the hull of a RIB, you will probably be able to travel to safety without too many problems. When you are on the plane, very little of the boat's hull is in contact with the water and so little water will come aboard. The danger, if you are stationary, is that the boat will fill up with water making it too heavy to lift back onto the plane. But you are unlikely to sink, as the tubes will support a flooded RIB.

Mending a punctured tube

The fabric that inflatable boats and RIB tubes are made of is straightforward to patch. The process is similar to mending a bicycle inner tube. For small holes a patch will be sufficient. For larger gashes, it may be better to stitch the edges together first to stabilise the area before applying a patch. Boat manufacturers will be able to give you the details of the fabric the boat is made from, what it can be patched with, and what glue to use.

- Pump up the tube and identify the hole by listening, feeling for the air leak or using soapy water.
- Deflate tube to avoid air disturbing the patch while the glue dries.
- Clean the fabric with an appropriate solvent, if advised to do so by the instructions for the glue.
- Roughen the surface of the fabric going under the patch.
- Apply the glue, according to the instructions. You may need more than one layer and it may need to dry to the touch before you apply the patch.
- Apply the patch, press firmly and avoid leaving any air bubbles underneath it. If it is large, work from one side to the other.
- Leave it to dry before pumping up the tube again.

However, if the hull of a rigid-hulled vessel, such as a dory, is damaged, it is important to act quickly. Such boats may not have enough inherent buoyancy to float when filled with water. If you can reach the hole, you can physically stem the flow, by holding something over it, and pump the bilges by every means possible.

Only abandon ship when it is absolutely necessary. A swamped vessel is much easier for the rescue services to find than a person. If you have to leave, transfer as much food and water into the life raft as you can and send a mayday call giving your sinking position (see *Distress calls*, page 99).

Fire

A fire onboard a vessel is a dangerous situation. The cause could be fuel-related, an electrical problem or something to do with your incendiary devices - that is flares. Any fire should be extinguished as quickly as possible. Fire needs heat, fuel and oxygen – remove any of these and the fire will be unable to burn.

Pleasure craft of less than 13.7 metres in length are not covered by any statutory requirements for fire fighting equipment. However, it is sensible to take some precautions against fire. RIBs should carry at least one multi-purpose, 2-kilogram fire extinguisher. Since December 2003, European Community regulations have prohibited the use of all halon fire extinguishers, which include the popular BCF extinguishers previously recommended for use on small boats. Dry powder or foam extinguishers are the most suitable extinguishers for small boats. They should have replaced all BCF extinguishers.

Water extinguishers are not suitable for fuel fires, as they can spread the liquid fuel and intensify the fire. They are also not suitable for mains-powered electrical fires, although where a 12-volt supply is used there is less chance of a harmful electric shock to the user. Water is useful to cool the embers of an extinguished fire.

All portable fire extinguishers should be maintained according to the manufacturer's instructions, which usually require periodic inspections and regular discharge and re-filling of devices.

It is worth making sure you and your divers and crew read and learn the operating instructions for your extinguishers, and keep all your equipment in good order. A few minutes planning and practising your fire drill could save lives and your vessel when every second counts. If you cannot put out the fire, and it is threatening the boat, you should send an immediate radio distress call.

Larger vessels tend to have a higher risk of explosion and fire than RIBs or inflatables. Gas cookers should be set up and operated carefully to avoid gas accumulating in the bilges and causing a fire hazard. Sniffer systems may be installed to give warning of unusually high gas levels in the bilges and other enclosed areas. Any fire, however small, should be extinguished as soon as possible using extinguishers or fire blankets. Many vessels have automatic fire-fighting systems installed especially in the engine room.

You should think about your own possible reactions to fire on board a charter vessel for example. Make sure you have read the operating instructions for the extinguishers. A few minutes planning and practising a fire drill could save life and the vessel when every second counts.

Helicopter rescues

Helicopter operations

Once you have summoned help, it is likely in UK waters that you will be attended to by either a lifeboat or a search and rescue helicopter. If a casualty requires evacuation by helicopter there are a number of things that you need to be aware of to safeguard yourself and the helicopter.

A hovering helicopter forces a column of air downwards. As this strikes the sea it initially moves outwards, creating a strong local wind, and then upwards. The downdraught will buffet a boat and its contents. Light objects can be lifted by the updraught, which could be hazardous to the helicopter. The downdraught also generates a lot of spray – to protect your eyes and maintain your vision, wear your diving facemask.

Communication is difficult below a hovering helicopter, as it is very noisy. It may be impossible to use a radio and communication with the helicopter may have to be by hand signals. There is also a great deal of static electricity generated by the helicopter. This can build up until a part of the helicopter touches the ground or sea surface, when it is all earthed. The winchman or the winch cable is likely to be the first thing to earth the static charge. Do not touch either until they have touched the boat or the sea, otherwise you will get an electric shock.

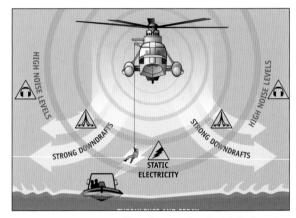

Hazards associated with helicopters

The helicopter pilot sits on the starboard side of the cockpit and has the maximum downward field of view on the starboard side of the nose. The pilot will usually ask the boat to head into the wind, with the wind 20 to 40 degrees off the port bow. This means the helicopter can fly into wind and have a good view of the boat. The helicopter's winch is also positioned on the starboard side.

Preparing for a lift
- Secure all loose objects
- Remove all obstructions, such as aerials
- Clear an area for the winchman to land in
- As the helicopter approaches, the boat will usually need to head to wind, with the wind 20 to 40 degrees off the port bow
- Maintain constant speed and heading
- Occupants of the boat should wear facemasks
- Winching operations are the responsibility of the helicopter crew. Watch for, and obey, their instructions

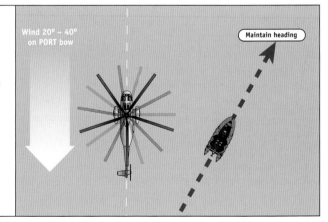

The direct lift can be used on all sizes of boat

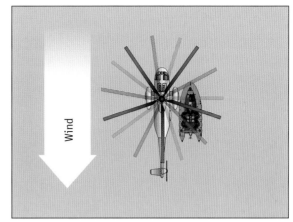

The alternative small boat technique requires the boat to remain stationary

Lifting methods

There are three types of lift likely to be used to evacuate a casualty. They are the direct lift; the high line transfer; and the alternative small boat technique.

To carry out a direct lift, the helicopter hovers above the boat and lowers the winchman directly onto the deck. This technique can be used on all sizes of boats. Remember not to touch the winchman before he, or the cable, has touched the deck.

In situations where obstructions on the boat cannot be removed or the boat's motion makes a direct lift difficult, a high line transfer may be used. In this technique a light line is dropped directly down to the boat. It will be used to guide the winchman onto the deck from the side. It must be kept free of all obstructions and not tied down to anything. Feeding it into a container such as a bucket will keep it tangle free and available. Once the boat crew have grabbed the line, the helicopter will move away to one side, paying out the line, and come to a low hover.

The winchman will be lowered, with the light line attached to the bottom of the winch cable. Keeping the winchman low over the water the helicopter will then resume a high hover and move back towards the boat. As the winchman approaches the boat, from the side, the slack in the light line should be taken up. Do not pull on the line. Once the winchman is only a few metres away, then tension on the line can be used to guide him over the deck. Eventually the winchman will board, with the

helicopter hovering slightly to port. If there is to be any delay, the helicopter may come to a low hover to the side of the boat again.

When ready to make the lift, the process is reversed. The helicopter will come in to a high hover over the boat again, and take up the slack in the cable. As the helicopter takes the weight of the winchman and casualty, it will lift them clear, moving to the side. The light line should be paid out with the minimum of slack. Once clear of the boat, the helicopter will come to a low hover and winch in the people. All that remains is to recover the light line. The helicopter will come to a high hover over the boat. When signalled to do so, you must let go of the end of the line, and it will be winched up into the helicopter.

With small boats, the helicopter crew may opt for a different procedure. The alternative small boat technique is a variation of the direct lift, for which the boat is requested to remain stationary. You will either be requested to deploy a sea anchor (see *Sea anchors*, page 110) or – if the conditions are right – to anchor. Divers should wear their facemasks. The helicopter will lower the winchman directly into the boat. Once the lift is completed, the boat can get underway again.

All of these techniques depend on the local conditions at the time, so be prepared to listen to and obey the instructions of the helicopter crew at all times.

Helicopter operations

High line transfer

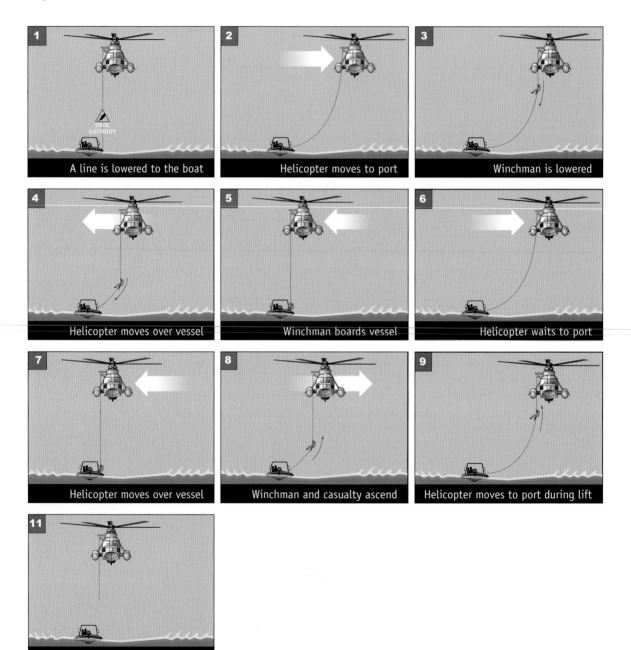

1. A line is lowered to the boat
2. Helicopter moves to port
3. Winchman is lowered
4. Helicopter moves over vessel
5. Winchman boards vessel
6. Helicopter waits to port
7. Helicopter moves over vessel
8. Winchman and casualty ascend
9. Helicopter moves to port during lift
11. Helicopter moves back over vessel, recovers line and departs

Chapter six

Voyage planning

In order to plan any voyage, you need to know: where you are, where you want to go to, what lies in your path, how your boat will cope and how the weather and the tides will affect your journey. All of this information, gathered from various sources, can then be put together in a practical plan to ensure a safe voyage.

SOLAS V

These common sense requirements for safe navigation and the avoidance of dangerous situations have become a legal requirement as summed up in regulation V/34 of Chapter V of the International Safety of Life at Sea convention. As a pleasure-boat user, you are required by SOLAS to carry out prior planning for any boat trip – known as voyage or passage planning. You should take into account the following points when planning your trip:

- Weather – before you leave you should check the weather forecast and get regular updates if you are planning to be out for any length of time.
- Tides – check the tidal predictions for your trip and ensure that they fit in with what you are planning.
- Limitations of the vessel – consider whether your boat is up to the trip and whether you have sufficient safety equipment and stores on board.
- Crew – take into account the experience and physical ability of your divers and crew.
- Navigational dangers – make sure you are familiar with any navigational dangers that you may encounter. This means checking an up-to-date chart and current pilot book or almanac.
- Contingency plan – always have a contingency plan should anything go wrong. Before you go, think of places to take refuge in should conditions deteriorate or an accident or injury occur. Bear in mind that your GPS set is vulnerable and could fail. It is sensible practice not to rely solely on your GPS, but to be able to navigate to safety by other means should it fail.
- Information ashore – make sure that someone ashore knows your plans and knows what to do should they become concerned about you.

VOYAGE PLANNING SHEET

DATE:		VOYAGE:	
COX'N:		DEPUTY COX'N:	
PASSENGERS:			

WEATHER FORECAST – INCLUDING SEA STATE:	AT LAUNCH:	UP TO 6 HOURS AFTER LAUNCH:

TIDES:	HIGH TIDE:		LOW TIDE:	
CURRENT:	OUTBOUND:	ON SITE:	INBOUND:	
HAZARDS:				

FUEL CHECKED:	ENGINE CHECKED:	BOAT CHECKED:
SAT. NAV. CHECKED:	ECHO SOUNDER CHECKED:	RADIO CHECKED:
OXYGEN CHECKED:	FIRST AID KIT CHECKED:	FLARES CHECKED:

VOYAGE DETAILS AFTER TAKING ALL OF THE ABOVE INTO CONSIDERATION:

SIGNED (COX'N):.. DATE:................................

(The Cox'n must also complete and sign the Boat Log Sheet overleaf)

A voyage planning sheet can be found on the BSAC website

Here we take a look at how to gather and interpret all the information needed to make a good voyage plan. A voyage-planning sheet can be used to note all relevant details for a proposed voyage.

Chart work

A chart is a map of an area of sea that gives more information about the sea and sea bed than it does about the land. Charts tell us about: the coastline, the topography of the land, buoyage, lights, dangers, depth of water, the quality of the sea bed, and tides and currents. Charts are available for most areas of the world, in different scales, and they are constantly updated. In the UK the largest publisher of marine charts is the United Kingdom Hydrographic Office. Other publishers produce charts for special interest groups, yachtsmen for example.

The scale of any chart is given underneath its title. This is the ratio of the length of any line measured on the chart to the corresponding line on the Earth's surface. A large-scale 1:25,000 chart has more detail than a small-scale 1:150,000 chart. On a 1:25,000 chart, one centimetre on the chart represents 25,000 centimetres on land, or 0.25 kilometres.

Diving trips should be planned using charts. As well as providing information about the dive site itself, charts enable you to plan a safe course to reach the dive site using landmarks or GPS waypoints, and to identify your position coordinates and alternative safe havens in case of emergency.

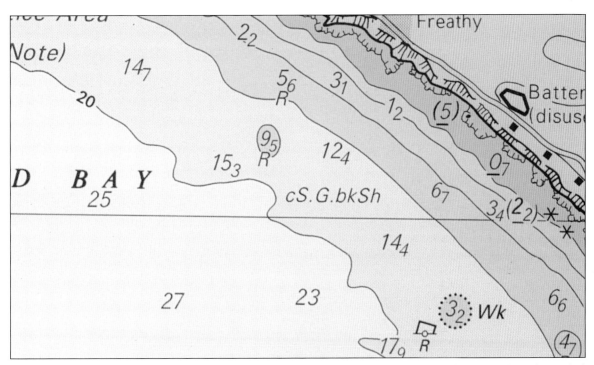

Charts give divers much detailed information about the sea bed

Fixing your position

Latitude and longitude: defining your position

The Earth can be thought of as a sphere that pivots about an axis. If the top end of the axis is the North Pole and the bottom end is the South Pole, the Earth rotates towards the east and away from the west.

Any point on Earth can be defined by measuring its distance from a vertical and horizontal reference point. These unique measurements are known as a position's coordinates. The midline drawn around the Earth, called the Equator, splits the Earth into the northern and southern hemispheres, and gives us a vertical reference point on the Earth. The horizontal reference point on Earth is the internationally agreed Greenwich meridian, which passes through the UK near London.

Lines of latitude are horizontal lines drawn parallel to the Equator. They are labelled in degrees north or south of the Equator, from 0 to 90, according to the angle that the line of latitude makes with the equator at the centre of the Earth. Lines of longitude (or meridians) are circumferences of the Earth that pass through, and intersect at, both poles. They are labelled in degrees east or west, from 0 to 180, according to the angle that they make with the Greenwich meridian at the centre of the Earth

Any position can, therefore, be identified by giving its latitude, suffixed by either north or south, followed by its longitude, suffixed by east or west. For example the UK port of Dover has coordinates of 51 degrees 06.74 minutes North, 001 degrees 19.73 minutes East.

One degree can be divided into 60 minutes. Minutes can be further divided into 60 seconds or, more commonly, decimal fractions of a second. Position should always be given as a six-figure coordinate, north or south, followed by a seven-figure coordinate, east or west.

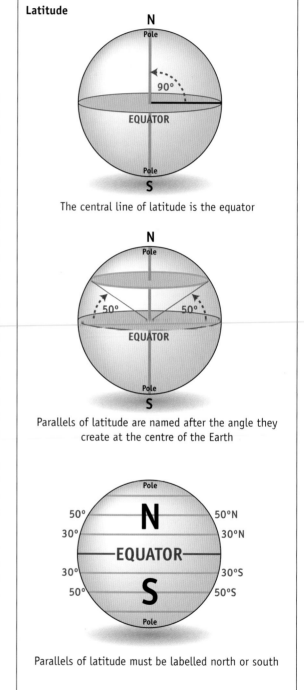

Latitude

The central line of latitude is the equator

Parallels of latitude are named after the angle they create at the centre of the Earth

Parallels of latitude must be labelled north or south

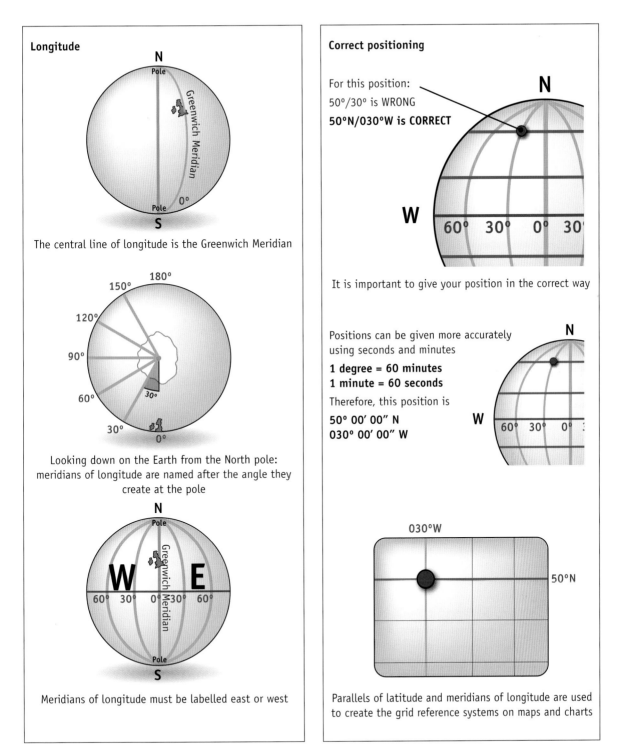

Longitude

The central line of longitude is the Greenwich Meridian

Looking down on the Earth from the North pole: meridians of longitude are named after the angle they create at the pole

Meridians of longitude must be labelled east or west

Correct positioning

For this position:
50°/30° is WRONG
50°N/030°W is CORRECT

It is important to give your position in the correct way

Positions can be given more accurately using seconds and minutes

1 degree = 60 minutes
1 minute = 60 seconds

Therefore, this position is

50° 00′ 00″ N
030° 00′ 00″ W

Parallels of latitude and meridians of longitude are used to create the grid reference systems on maps and charts

Types of chart

Types of chart

Since the Earth is a sphere, its surface is curved. But maps and charts are flat. Translating the curved surface of the Earth onto a flat piece of paper can be done in several mathematical ways, or projections, each of which distorts some aspect of the area under consideration.

The most useful type of projection used to create a chart is the Mercator projection. This represents lines of longitude as straight, parallel, equally spaced, vertical lines and lines of latitude as straight, parallel, horizontal lines. The lines of latitude are not equally spaced: the latitude scale gradually increases as you move away from the Equator in either direction.

This means that to measure distance on a Mercator chart you must consult the latitude, or vertical, scale in the area of the chart that you are working in. You cannot use the longitude, or horizontal, scale to measure distance.

The regular grid of a Mercator chart is easy to use for position fixing. The start and finish of a journey can be joined by a straight line, from which we can determine the distance to travel and the direction of travel.

The other type of chart projection in use, particularly for polar regions, large oceans and harbour plans, is the gnomonic projection. Such projections have converging, straight lines of longitude and curved lines of latitude. The shortest distance between two points on the Earth's surface on a gnomonic chart gives what is known as a 'great circle route', which ships can use to save fuel.

A small-scale gnomonic chart will have lines of longitude that converge towards the poles and lines of latitude that curve. However on large-scale gnomonic charts, such as harbours plans, the grid will appear to be parallel and the chart can be used like any other. Distance can be measured either by using the latitude scale as is done on Mercator charts, or using the separate scale of distance that is marked at the bottom or side of the chart.

Measuring distance at sea

The nautical mile is used to measure distance at sea. This is defined as the distance, measured along a line of longitude, which separates two points whose latitude varies by exactly one minute of arc at the centre of the Earth, that is one-sixtieth of a degree. This is usually taken to be 1852 metres or 6080 feet, or 115 per cent of a statute mile.

Because the nautical mile is defined in terms of minutes of latitude, it is easy to measure distance on a chart. You simply measure a distance, usually by using dividers to span two points on the chart, and then see how many minutes that distance spans on the latitude scale of the chart at that particular latitude. The number of minutes equals the number of nautical miles.

Charts may also have a separate scale of distance marked at one edge, in either nautical miles or kilometres or both. This can also be used to measure distance. Do not use the longitude (horizontal) scale to measure distance on any chart.

Speed at sea is measured in knots. One knot is equal to one nautical mile per hour.

Information given on charts

Charts are crammed with various types of information. To understand the symbols and abbreviations that are used to save space on the chart you will need to consult *Chart 5011*. This is a booklet containing a comprehensive list of all the symbols and abbreviations used on Admiralty charts.

Charts show the depth of water that can be expected, either as individual soundings or depth contours, linking points of the same depth. All current UK charts give depths in metres, measured above chart datum. This datum is set as the level below which the tide will rarely if ever fall. As a diver, you may find that the depth reading from the chart does not exactly correspond to the depth of your dive. It will depend where you are in the daily and

Abbreviations used on charts
The quality of the sea bed

S	sand	M	mud	
Sn	shingle	St	stones	
R	rock	Wd	weed	
f	fine	c	coarse	
bk	broken	so	soft	

Dangers

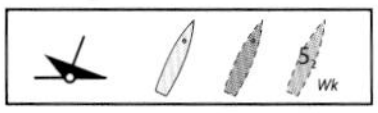

		Wk	wreck
Bk	bank	Rf	reef
Le	ledge		

rock which does not cover

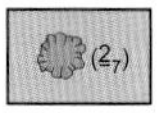

rock which covers and uncovers

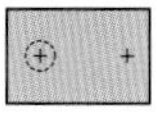

+ underwater rock, generally with less than 2m water over it

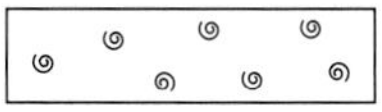

eddies

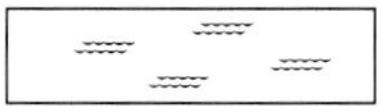

overfalls

Surface topography

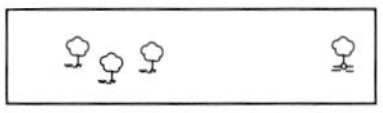

deciduous, evergreen, unknown trees

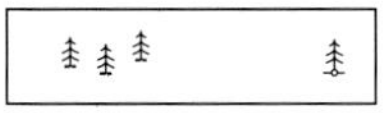

coniferous trees

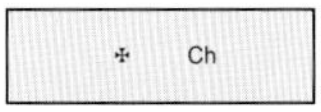

church/chapel

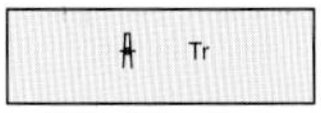

tower

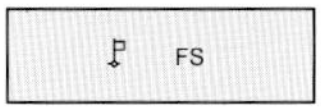

flagstaff

Buoys and beacons (IALA A system)

buoyage direction

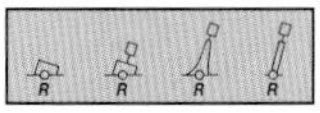

port hand lateral marks

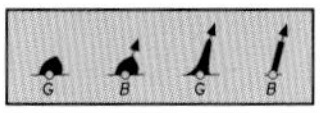

starboard hand lateral marks

Lights

position of important light

How some of these appear on a chart

Prominent features

Dry land – yellow

Areas that cover/uncover with tide – green

Sea areas mainly white but shallow areas solid blue or edged in blue

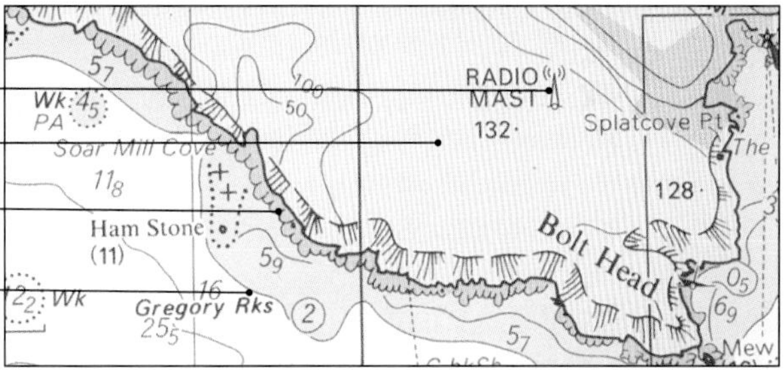

Depth contour lines

Type of seabed

Depth soundings

Obstruction

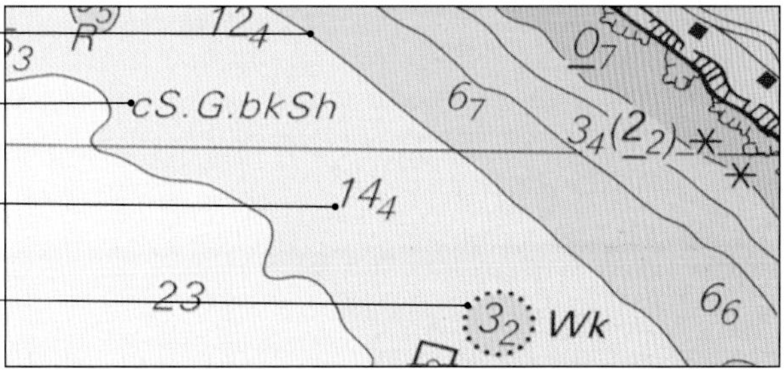

Chart symbols

monthly tidal cycle (see *Measuring the tide*, page 142).

Sometimes depths are shown with a symbol underneath that resembles a square bracket lying on its back. These tend to occur in areas where an underwater object would be a considerable danger to shipping and indicate that the depth was established by sweeping the area with a wire drag. This tells us that the site is clear to the depth shown, it does not always tell divers the actual depth of the feature, which could be deeper.

Chart datum is always stated underneath the title of the chart. On some older charts it may still be a physical datum such as a mark on a harbour wall. If you use the depth information given on a chart correctly, there should rarely be less water than the depth shown.

The foreshore and rocks and banks that uncover are coloured green on charts. Underlined figures shown on these express heights above the datum of the chart. These are known as drying heights. They will be the maximum height of the feature, not necessarily the height that you will see on any day.

The chart also gives information about the nature of the sea bed at any particular point. This information is useful to divers, as it may reveal much about the underwater conditions. It also gives you an idea of how successfully you could anchor.

Dangers to navigation, which are often sites of interest to divers, are shown on the chart. They range from tides, eddies and currents to rocks, wrecks and reefs.

The surface topography of the land will help with navigation and position fixing. Conspicuous features such as church towers, steeples, castles and prominent masts are shown. Fixed lights and beacons are marked with information about their colour, their pattern and frequency and the distance over which they can be seen.

The positions of navigational buoys are shown, together with their markings and the type of warning they carry. They are useful as way points but not for position fixing as they are fixed to the sea bed by a sinker and chain,

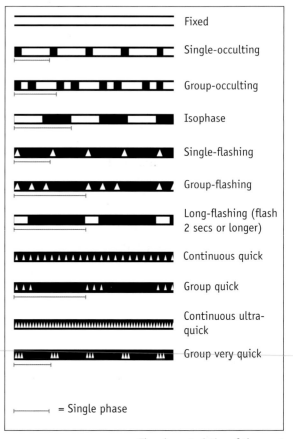

The characteristics of the most common lights

which has to allow for the rise and fall of the tide. Thus they can move position, depending on the state of the tide and the direction of the wind and current.

Using a compass

A compass is an extremely simple device. A magnetic compass consists of a small, lightweight magnet balanced on a nearly frictionless pivot point, above a card. The magnet or needle is usually coloured or marked N for north at the end that points north. Ships' compasses are set up in fluid-filled spheres that allow them to remain horizontal even when the boat is moving. You must take care with hand-held compasses to keep them horizontal. If the needle rubs

The theory of calculating compass error

On every chart there is at least one compass rose. This usually takes the form of a circle graduated from 0 to 360 degrees in a clockwise direction. Bearings and courses are always given as three digit numbers. For example: north is 000 degrees (or 360 degrees); east is 090 degrees; south is 180 degrees; and west is 270 degrees.

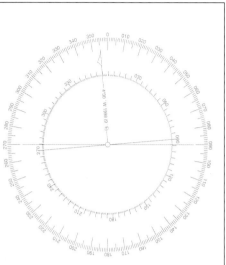

- Most compass roses have an inner circle, which can be used to automatically allow for the variation between true north and compass north, in that area on a fixed date. There is also a correction factor to be applied to calculate variation on later dates.
- If variation is increasing annually, you must add the correct number of years of annual change to the variation.
- If variation is decreasing annually, you must subtract the correct number of years of annual change from the variation.
- Then you can use the variation to correct a bearing taken from the chart.
- To account for deviation for any heading, you can read the expected deviation from the Deviation Card and apply it (page 128).
- Total compass error takes into account both variation and deviation. You must add the figures if they are in the same direction and subtract the figures if they are in opposite directions.
- Once compass error is known you will be able to convert a compass reading to a true reading by either adding or subtracting the compass error. A convenient way of doing this is to remember, 'Error west, compass best. Error east, compass least'. In other words if the compass error is west, the compass reading will be greater than the true reading. If the compass error is east then the compass reading should be less than the true reading.
- When plotting positions and courses on a chart, only true readings should be used.

on the card, the friction will affect the reading.

The card on a compass can be marked in a number of ways, all of which indicate direction. The simplest and most accurate method is the three-figure method. Here the compass card is divided into 360 degrees, moving clockwise from north which is 000 degrees, through 090 degrees (east), 180 degrees (south) and 270 degrees (west). Direction is always described using three figures.

The point method divides the circle into 32 equal parts or points. A full circle is 360 degrees, so each point represents 11.25 degrees.

The quadrantal method marks the card into four quadrants each divided into 90 degrees, with zero at north and south, and 90 at east and west. The cardinal directions are described simply as north, south, east and west. Intermediate directions are described from north or south towards east or west: north west becomes N 45 degrees W.

Compass error

Compasses are subject to two types of error: one is due to the nature of the Earth, the other is due to the nature of the compass.

True north on Earth is defined as the upper point of the Earth's axis. However, a magnetic compass used for navigation, and under no other influences, will point to magnetic north. Magnetic north and true north do not usually coincide. The difference between them is called variation. The value of the variation changes from place to place on the Earth's surface, and it changes with time.

Compass error

On small dive boats that can only hold their course to within plus or minus 10 degrees, you may not need to allow for variation when using a compass. But for larger vessels, travelling longer distances, variation becomes much more important. It is possible to calculate variation from the chart.

A magnetic compass will also suffer a second error called deviation. This is caused by the presence of other magnetic influences, such as steel items and electrical gear. A compass suffering from deviation will not read true north or magnetic north, but it will show what is called compass north. If you are using a portable compass, you can simply move away from the magnetic influence. If you are using a fixed compass on board a larger vessel then, for accurate navigation, you will need to know the deviation due to the vessel and its cargo. On larger vessels you may see a deviation card, which can be used to correct for deviation.

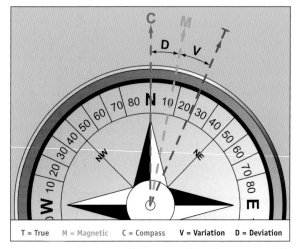

T = True   M = Magnetic   C = Compass   V = Variation   D = Deviation

True, magnetic and compass north

A console-mounted compass

An example of a calculation of variation

If the chart states that the variation was 12 degrees W in 2000 and is decreasing 10 minutes annually then to calculate the actual variation in 2005, five years after the variation reading was taken, you will have to do the following sum: (12 degrees W) minus (5 x 10 minutes). So, the variation would be 11 degrees and 10 minutes W in 2005.

This means that in 2005, a true bearing of 90 degrees taken from this chart would be corrected by adding 11 degrees and 10 minutes W to it to make a compass bearing of 101 degrees and 10 minutes.

Examples of the calculation of total compass error		
Variation	Deviation	Compass error
7 degrees W	10 degrees W	17 degrees W
7 degrees W	10 degrees E	3 degrees E
7 degrees E	10 degrees W	3 degrees W
7 degrees E	10 degrees E	17 degrees E

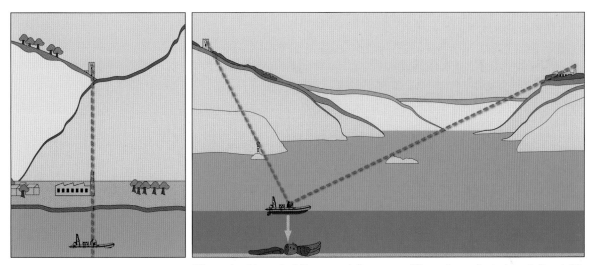

Where should you be? You cannot fix your position using a single transit (top left).
Two transits will give a position fix (top right)

Position fixing

You need to know where you are at sea, and this is what position fixing is all about. It is possible to obtain a position fix in several ways using transits and compass bearings or with electronic navigation aids such as GPS and radar, if fitted. In a small dive boat, you are unlikely to want to plot positions on the chart while at sea, but information prepared in advance can be transferred to a slate and used to find a dive site, for example. On a larger boat, there may be a chart table and navigational instruments to work with.

A 'position line' is a line on the chart on which a boat's position is known to be. A 'position fix', which defines exactly where a vessel is, is obtained when two or more position lines cross. A 'cocked hat' is created when three or more position lines do not quite line up. Providing the area of the cocked hat is not too large, it can still be used to determine your position. If your transits are too close together, then the area of uncertainty will increase.

Using transits

When two objects are observed in line, they are said to be in transit. This type of position line is also called a fisherman's mark. If the distance between the observer and the nearest mark is not more than about three times the distance separating the two objects, the method can be quite accurate. It is a popular method for finding a dive site: a set of three transits is ideal. If you are already on site, you can take transits to enable you to find it again. Or if you are given transits for a known site, you can use those to find it yourself.

To use a pair of transits to position a boat, it is best to steer towards the objects along one transit until the second, and third, come into line. If you quickly mark your position, then you can check it at your leisure.

Taking a bearing

A bearing on a visible object can be taken with a hand-bearing compass or with the boat's compass. This will be a magnetic bearing unless you allow for compass error to calculate a true bearing.

Bearing can be used in conjunction with transits to find a dive site, as they tell you in which direction to look to find a particular mark. You can take a magnetic bearing from a chart in advance and use it to get yourself roughly into position at sea. If you use one bearing you will only be able to fix your position to somewhere along that position line. Using two bearings will give you a rough fix.

Try to take a hand-bearing compass well away from any magnetic influences such as steel fittings and electrical equipment when you want to take a reading: this will

Using transits

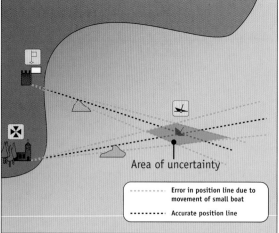

The area of uncertainty surrounding a position fixed using two transits that are close together is large

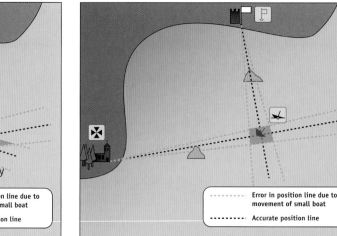

Two sets of transits should be about 90° apart to give an accurate position

In both diagrams:
- ········· Error in position line due to movement of small boat
- ▪▪▪▪▪▪▪▪▪ Accurate position line

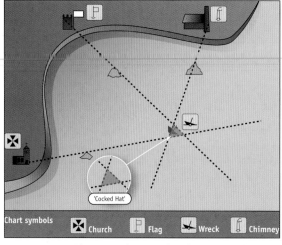

Three transits can give rise to a 'cocked hat'

Chart symbols: ✠ Church ⚑ Flag ⚓ Wreck ⌂ Chimney

Using a hand-held compass

minimise deviation. Hold the compass up to your eyes and, keeping it horizontal, point it at the object whose bearing you want to take. Wait for the needle to stop swinging before you take a reading.

You will need to stop the boat to take a compass bearing. In anything other than a flat calm sea, the boat becomes an unstable platform and it is difficult to take an accurate bearing. In an emergency, if your boat electronics are out of action, you may want to take a bearing on a visible object and give that information, along with an estimated distance from the object, to the coastguard.

Finding a course to steer
A dive boat may reach its destination by starting at a fixed point and following a compass bearing, or by pilotage, that is using obvious landmarks to travel along a true course.

Electronic navigation aids

RIBs and purpose-built charter boats usually have a power supply available and this gives divers the opportunity to make use of electronic navigation aids such as echo sounders, moving maps and electronic charts. Early navigation systems such as the radio position fixing system Decca were expensive and could be temperamental. Today the Global Positioning System (GPS) provides a highly accurate, worldwide, continuous, three-dimensional (latitude, longitude and altitude) position fixing system in all weather conditions. It can offer accuracy to within three to five metres. It is a readily available, competitively priced tool even for small dive boats, but like all electrics at sea it is not wise to rely on it totally and forget the more basic methods of position fixing.

Global Positioning System

GPS is based on a system of up to 30 satellites, each of which continuously broadcasts its position and the time of day. Radio waves travel at a constant speed of about 162,000 nautical miles per second. Thus a GPS receiver, knowing the time the radio signal was sent and the time the signal arrives at the set, can calculate how far away it is from the satellite. Knowing the exact positions of the satellites, the receiver can obtain a position fix using signals from several satellites, in the same way that you carry out a manual position fix.

The high speed of the signals means that an error in the receiver's clock of even only a few milliseconds could affect the position fix by miles. But by using signals from extra satellites, a GPS receiver can adjust its clock continuously and give a position fix to within 20 metres. Most current GPS sets are parallel receivers, with up to twelve channels. Six channels would give sufficient accuracy for small boats.

Differential GPS (dGPS) can give an accuracy of within three to five metres. This automated system uses reference stations to transmit corrections to be applied to the satellite signals. These corrections are different to

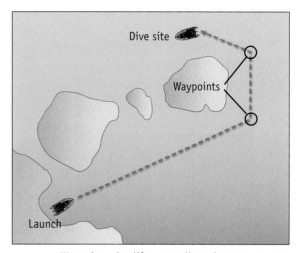
Waypoints simplify a complicated course to steer

GPS signals themselves and to receive them you need a differential beacon receiver. This can be integrated into a GPS or it could be a separate black box designed to enhance the performance of an existing set.

The Wide Area Augmentation System, WAAS, is the latest development in GPS technology. In the US the system is up and running. A European version called EGNOS is expected soon. Position accuracy is around three metres and WAAS does not need a separate antenna.

As well as giving you an instant position fix, all GPS receivers can store planned positions as waypoints. If you enter a waypoint, the set will tell you the direction and distance to travel to reach that spot. Also, the set can calculate your speed and direction of travel. Because it reduces positioning errors, differential GPS improves the accuracy of this speed and direction information considerably.

Depending on the sophistication of the GPS set, it is possible to display this information either as a basic, real-time moving map, or as graphic highway steering guidance, or to superimpose it onto an electronic chart.

Electronic navigation aids

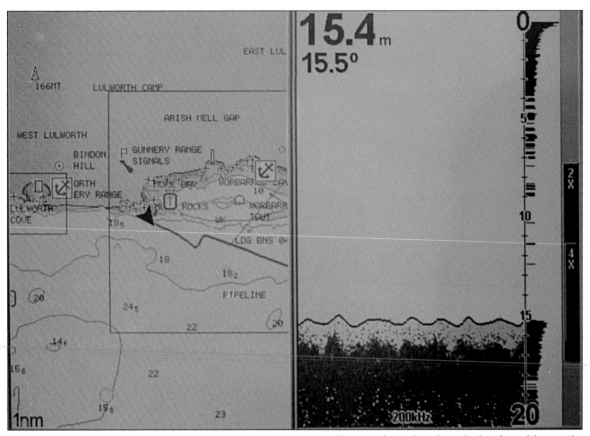

A split screen is used to show the boat's position on the chart and an echo sounder trace

Electronic charts are invaluable tools not only for position fixing, but also for finding dive sites. It is possible to zoom in to show as much detail about the sea bed as you would find on a paper chart. There are two broad classes of chart available – raster and vector charts. Different GPS hardware manufacturers have adopted different brands of electronic chart. You will need to get up-to-date, expert advice before committing to a system.

GPS satellites are referenced to the World Geodetic System 84 (WGS84) datum. This means that satellite fixes cannot be directly plotted onto nautical charts, which are often still referenced to a local datum. Corrections need to be applied to get the full benefit of the precision of GPS positions. Correction information is given on the chart, in a note called 'satellite derived positions', usually found near to the chart's title block. The UK Hydrographic Office is in the process of converting all UK charts to the WGS84 datum. This process should have been completed in 2004. You should be aware that the chart datum and GPS datum may not be the same. Good GPS sets allow the user to select from a choice of different datums.

GPS receivers are often found combined with an echo sounder in one unit. These are easy to use and save space on a small boat's console. They can often be set to split the screen and display information about the sea bed as well as your position on an electronic chart. The disadvantage of such units is that if either part fails you lose both while a repair is carried out.

Radar

Radar operates by sending out short pulses of super high frequency radiation (microwaves), which are focused into a narrow beam by a rotating antenna. Pulses reflected back from the leading edge of solid objects are collected, amplified and processed to give a direction to, and distance from, the object. In this way, a trace is built up of a vessel's surroundings. Radar is almost universal in larger vessels as it gives valuable security in heavy weather, at night and off unfamiliar coasts.

The effective range of radar is line of sight. It suffers from the drawback that it cannot differentiate between two objects that are close together. Also, objects with sharp features give better reflections than curved shapes – thus cliffs give a good signal but a low-lying coastline may be invisible to radar. There is a system of radar beacons, Racons, which are used for coastal navigation of larger vessels.

Unlike older sets, where the screen had to be viewed through a deep, light-tight cowl, modern radar systems use liquid-crystal displays, visible in bright daylight. They can be set up to share the same screen as chart plotters and echo sounders – each selected by the user when appropriate.

As many large ships rely on radar for navigation and for spotting other vessels in their vicinity, whatever the size of your boat, it is important to make sure that you can be seen by radar. Regulation V/19 of the International Convention for the Safety of Life at Sea (SOLAS), requires all small craft to carry radar reflectors if practicable. If your boat is more than 15 metres in length you should fit a radar reflector that meets the International Maritime Organisation standard of 10 m² If your boat is less than 15 metres long, you should fit the largest reflector that you can. The reflector should be fitted according to the manufacturer's instructions and as high as possible on your boat to maximise its effectiveness.

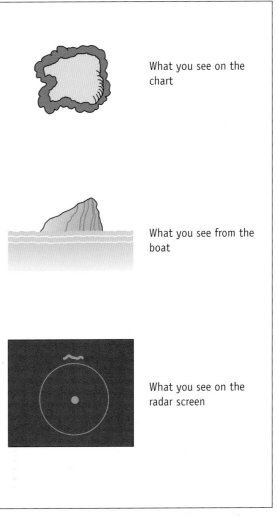

What you see on the chart

What you see from the boat

What you see on the radar screen

The picture on a radar screen is not a simple map

Echo sounders

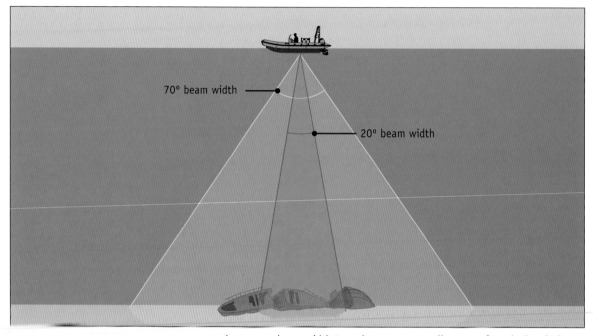

A narrower beam width transducer sees a smaller area of sea bed and gives a more accurate picture

Echo sounders

Although echo sounders do not give any position information they are used in conjunction with transits or GPS positions to confirm the underwater profile at the site. The principle of echo sounding is simple. A pulse of sound is emitted by a transducer, which is attached to the hull of a boat, for example. The pulse of sound is reflected back from the sea bed and the time taken for the return journey gives a measure of depth. From the display it is possible to determine some characteristics of the sea bed and shoals of fish can also be detected.

The quality of the information available depends in part on the type of transducer used. In shallow water, a wide beam angle of up to 70 degrees can be used to cover a large area of sea bed and will give adequate definition. But the same transducer used in deeper water will lose power and the fine detail of the topography may be lost. For divers wanting good definition in depths of 20 to 50 metres of water, a narrower beam angle of 20 degrees means that the power is more concentrated and the bottom resolution is much improved. With a beam angle of eight degrees, the instrument is sampling only a 2 metre wide section of sea bed at a depth of 15 metres or a 7-metre section of sea bed at 50 metres.

An echo sounder for use on a small dive boat should have a clear display in a waterproof unit. Alarms for both shallow and deep water can be useful.

Echo sounder traces require some thought to analyse or you can be easily misled. The apparent slope of the ground, as shown on the trace, will depend on the speed of the pass over the sea bed. If the boat is moving slowly, the trace will appear to show a shallower slope than it would if the boat was moving faster over the same area of sea bed. Moving ahead too fast and moving in reverse can both lead to misleading traces as air bubbles mixed in with the water can give a confused signal.

Standard moving map and echo sounder trace

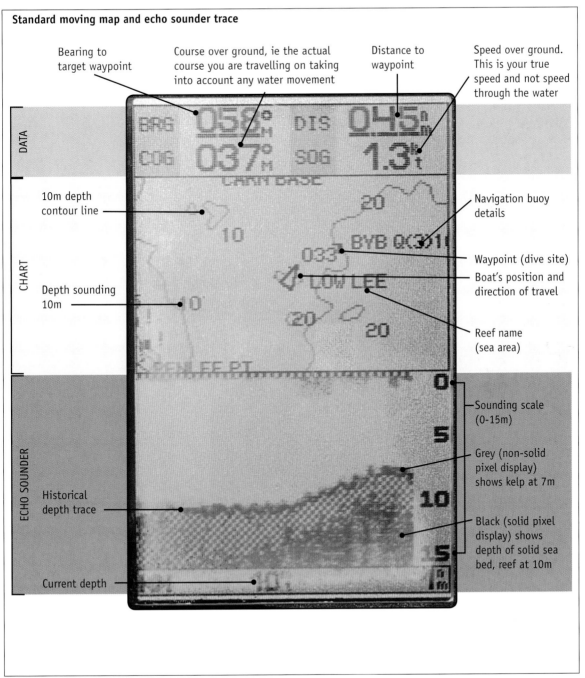

Bearing to target waypoint

Course over ground, ie the actual course you are travelling on taking into account any water movement

Distance to waypoint

Speed over ground. This is your true speed and not speed through the water

DATA

BRG 058°m

DIS 0.45 n m

COG 037°m

SOG 1.3 kt

CHART

10m depth contour line

Navigation buoy details

Depth sounding 10m

Waypoint (dive site)

Boat's position and direction of travel

Reef name (sea area)

ECHO SOUNDER

Historical depth trace

Current depth

Sounding scale (0-15m)

Grey (non-solid pixel display) shows kelp at 7m

Black (solid pixel display) shows depth of solid sea bed, reef at 10m

Interpreting echo sounder traces

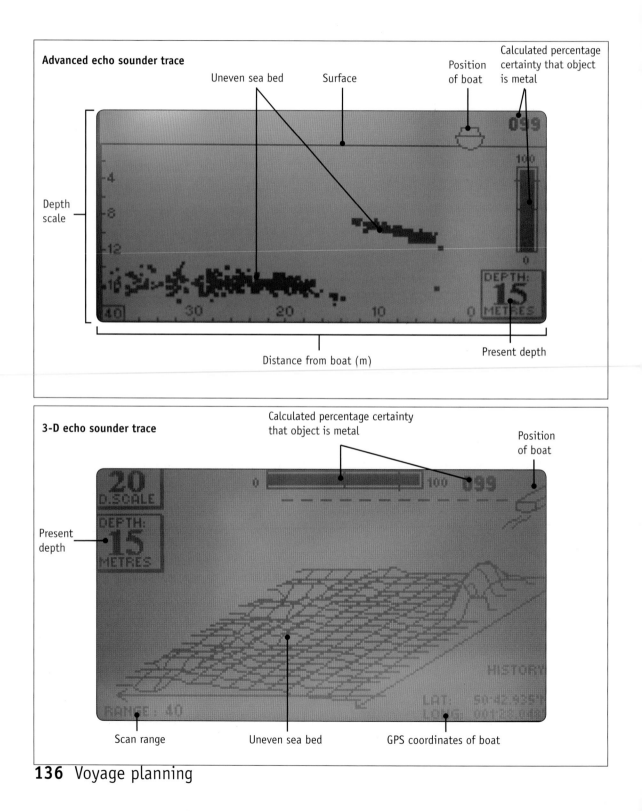

Advanced echo sounder trace

Uneven sea bed

Surface

Position of boat

Calculated percentage certainty that object is metal

099

100

0

Depth scale

4

8

12

16

40

30

20

10

0

DEPTH: **15** METRES

Distance from boat (m)

Present depth

3-D echo sounder trace

Calculated percentage certainty that object is metal

0   100   099

Position of boat

20 D.SCALE

Present depth

DEPTH: **15** METRES

RANGE: 40

HISTORY

LAT: 50 42 935'
LONG: 00123 042

Scan range

Uneven sea bed

GPS coordinates of boat

Tactics of site location

The prevalence of electronic navigation aids in small dive boats means it can be relatively easy to return to the same dive site again and again. But sometimes you will want to find a new site, either from someone else's description or some other source. How to locate a position on a stretch of water really depends on your surroundings. In the open sea, or off a flat and featureless coastline, electronic position fixing is the only practical option. However rocky shores provide more opportunity for the use of transits.

Searches

Once you have located the general area, using a position fix or a set of transits, you will need to carry out some type of search either to monitor the topography of the sea bed with an echo sounder or to look for magnetic anomalies with a proton magnetometer, for example. The tactics of searching are really common sense. You need an initial reference point or datum, for which you can use a marker buoy. Then you will need to search the area around it. This could be done using a circular sweep at increasing distances around the datum. Or you could work backwards and forwards in a predetermined grid pattern. Further buoys can be used to mark areas searched or items of interest.

During your search it makes sense to use tide and wind to best effect. Once you have made initial contact with the site, extra sweeps with an echo sounder for example will give you a great deal of useful information. With small boats it is necessary to move slowly when echo sounding to avoid false echoes caused by the turbulence around the transducer. If you have some information about the way a wreck is lying for example, you may well be able to place shot-lines to dive specific areas such as the bow or stern.

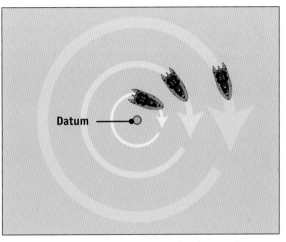

A circular search pattern

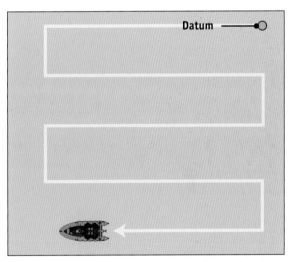

A grid search pattern

Proton magnetometer

These instruments measure the Earth's magnetic field. The high concentration of ferrous material in a shipwreck for example will distort this field and that will be detected by the proton magnetometer. Units need to be tuned for a particular locality before beginning a search. Planning your search grid in an east-west direction gives the best results as the Earth's magnetic lines of force are being crossed at 90 degrees.

Marking the site

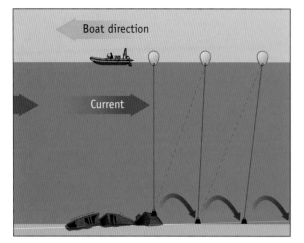

When manoevering up current, a shot deployed as the echo sounder trace begins to show the wreck is likely to drift

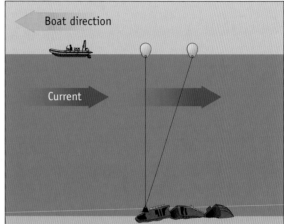

A shot deployed as the echo sounder trace begins to fall away after the wreck is likely to remain on site

Sonar

Sonar uses the principle of echo sounding, but with more complicated electronics that give a graduated response to the pulse echoes. The area of sweep can extend from several hundred metres to about two miles either side of the vessel. Sonar gives a picture of the sea bed with a resolution similar to a low-resolution photograph. Sea bed features are shown in great detail. Sonar is often seen in documentaries about wreck finding. It is the tool of choice of professional wreck finders and is expensive.

Marking the site

When marking a site it is useful to have a dedicated person ready with the shot-line. You can then motor up to the site, using transits or the echo sounder, and coordinate bringing the boat to a stop and dropping the shot. If you want to deploy a shot-line when a current is running, you will need to take extra care to get it on site. If you head into the tide, and deploy the shot as soon as you see the feature on the echo sounder it is likely that you will drift back in neutral as the shot descends and it will land downstream of the site. Also, any effect of the tide will push it further off site.

It is much better to head into the current and wait until the site is clearly seen on the echo sounder and you are beginning to move away on the other side, before you drop the weight any effect of the current will tend to move it back onto the site. Finally, using transits or the GPS position, you should check that the shot is not drifting because the line is too short, or dragging because the weight is too light. If you think the shot is not on the site, recover it and start the process again.

On a busy site, it is good practice to keep to a minimum your movements over the main part of the site. Other boats will be dropping off and picking up divers, all in a small area. Sometimes it may not be possible to drop a shot-line of your own, for fear of hitting other divers with it. In this case, ask to use one of the existing shots. It will be appreciated by others, if your divers understand that they should not pull on the shot line, which could displace it, but merely use it to guide themselves to the site.

To recover a shot-line, you can either haul it in, which can be hard work, or use a lifting bag to raise the weight. As one litre of water weighs one kilogram, you will need one litre of air to lift each kilogram of shot weight. A 25-kilogram shot weight will therefore need a 25-litre lifting bag to raise it in a controlled lift. In this case, the

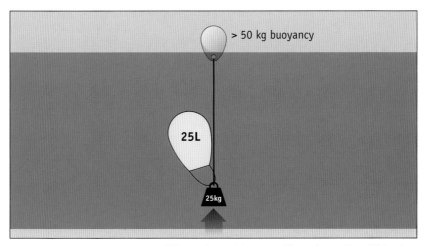

> 50 kg buoyancy

25L

25kg

To lift a 25 kg weight you will need a 25 litre lifting bag

last pair of divers to ascend the shot, fill the lifting bag and the weight becomes neutrally buoyant, or slightly negative. They can then complete their ascent. The buoy and line are recovered after all the divers are aboard. The effort to raise the weight will be minimal as the lifting bag will start to spill air as the weight rises, but will always have enough buoyancy to conteract the weight.

Using a lifting bag that has more buoyancy than needed to raise the weight will result in a buoyant lift. The last pair of divers to use the shotline, should fill the lifting bag enough to just lift the weight, making sure that they are well clear of the whole assembly. Then the addition of a little bit more air will start the buoyant lift. The divers should then move away from below the ascent path of the weight. The boat should also stay well clear until the lifting bag surfaces, in order to avoid entanglement in the line.

As a shot-line is recovered it should be flaked, buoy end first, back into its container, to avoid tangles. The weight can be kept on top of the line, as it is deployed first.

When you are searching a general area, bear in mind that there are visual signs that can indicate the presence of an irregular feature on the sea bed. A surface disturbance such as local waves, or tidal stream diversions can indicate an underwater obstruction to the current flow. To see these best you will need to be on site while any current is still running. Depending on the underwater visibility, you may see changes in the colour of the water over a wreck. Visible, shallow weed in otherwise deep water indicates shallow ground.

Tides

Tides

Tides are the periodic movements of the sea mainly in response to the pull of the moon and the sun on the water. In the UK, tides are usually semi-diurnal – that is there are two high waters and two low waters in each lunar day. A lunar day is about 24 hours and 50 minutes. The difference in height of the water between two successive high and low waters is called the range of the tide. In the UK the tidal range can vary from as little as one metre to as much as 10 metres. The time between successive high waters is called the duration of the tide. It is about half a lunar day or 12 hours and 24 minutes. Close to land, the movements of the sea can become complex as they are affected not only by the pull of the sun and moon but also by local underwater topography. Detailed tidal flow information can be found on charts, in tidal stream atlases or in tidal stream charts in almanacs.

The greatest range of the tide is found at or near the new or full moon, as it is then that the Earth, sun and moon are aligned. These are called spring tides and they occur about every 15 days. If the moon and sun are aligned on the same side of the Earth, they exert the greatest force on the water, causing the highest spring tides.

About seven and a half days after the new or full moon, the sun and moon are at right angles to each other and the smallest range of tides is found at this time. These are called neap tides and they also occur every 15 days, just after the half moons.

As you move between spring and neap tides, the high-water heights gradually decrease and the low-water heights gradually increase, thus decreasing the tidal range. Between neaps and springs the opposite occurs: high-water heights increase and low-water heights decrease to increase the tidal range.

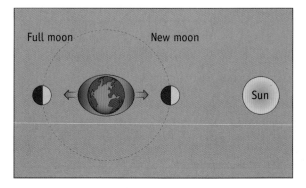

Spring tide means higher high tides and lower low tides

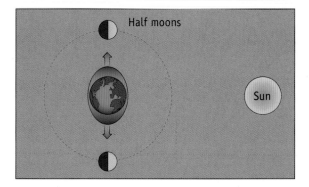

Neap tide means lower high tides and higher low tides

Talking about tides

Chart datum – the level below which the tide will rarely, if ever fall. Used to measure the depth to the sea bed on charts.

Height of the tide – the height of the sea's surface above chart datum at any time

High water – the highest level reached by the sea's surface during any one tidal cycle

Low water – the lowest level reached by the sea's surface during any one tidal cycle

Range of the tide – the difference in height between high and low water for one tidal cycle

Spring tides – tides of maximum range

Neap tides – tides of minimum range

Equinoctial spring tides – greater than average spring tides occurring near the spring and autumn equinoxes

Mean high-water springs (MHWS) – average height of high water at spring tides, used to measure the height of land objects shown on the chart

Mean low-water springs (MLWS) – average height of low water at spring tides

Mean high-water neaps (MHWN) – average height of high water at neap tides

Mean low-water neaps (MLWN) – average height of low water at neap tides

Highest astronomical tide (HAT) – highest predictable tide under average meteorological conditions

Lowest astronomical tide (LAT) – lowest predictable tide under average meteorological conditions

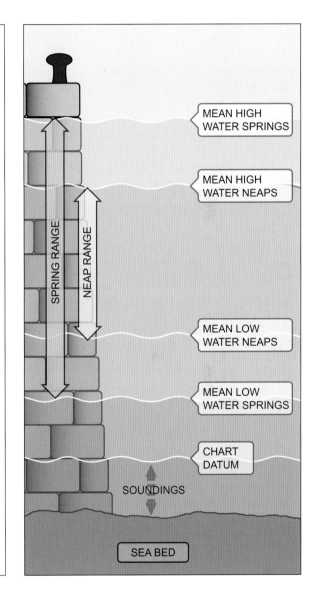

Tide tables

Measuring the tide

The UK Hydrographic Office publishes tide tables every year, to predict the times and heights of high and low water every day at certain important 'standard' ports. Correction information is also given in the tide tables to enable calculation of times and heights of high and low water at a wider range of 'secondary' ports.

Note that all tidal heights given in tidal information are heights above chart datum. When calculating the depth of water at a dive site it is necessary to allow for the stage of the tidal cycle and the state of the tide, because an error of even a few metres will inconvenience mixed gas divers and others restricted to certain depths.

Having found the tidal range for a particular day at a particular site, the depth of water at any particular time can be calculated. One method is to estimate the depth using the rule of twelfths (see opposite).

JULY 2004

Adjusted for G.M.T. and British Summer Time. Height in meters (1 metre = 3ft)

DATE	DAY	HIGH WATER Morning Time	Ht m	Afternoon Time	Ht m	LOW WATER Morning Time	Ht m	Afternoon Time	Ht m
1	Th	4 37	6.6	5 04	6.8	11 08	1.1	11 33	0.9
2	F Ω	5 31	6.8	5 57	7.0	11 58	0.9		
3	Sa	6 24	6.9	6 46	7.2	00 25	0.7	12 48	0.8
4	Su	7 15	7.0	7 38	7.2	1 18	0.6	1 38	0.8
5	M	8 06	6.9	8 28	7.1	2 10	0.6	2 30	0.9
6	Tu	8 54	6.7	9 17	6.9	3 01	0.8	3 19	1.1
7	W	9 43	6.4	10 06	6.6	3 51	1.0	4 07	1.4
8	Th	10 31	6.1	10 56	6.2	4 40	1.3	4 58	1.8
9	F	11 21	5.8	11 50	6.0	5 30	1.8	5 50	2.1
10	Sa	** **	***	12 19	5.6	6 25	2.1	6 51	2.3
11	Su	00 51	5.7	1 23	5.4	7 24	2.3	7 55	2.4
12	M	1 53	5.6	2 27	5.5	8 25	2.4	9 00	2.4
13	Tu	2 56	5.6	3 28	5.6	9 25	2.3	9 57	2.3
14	W	3 53	5.8	4 18	5.9	10 16	2.1	10 45	2.1
15	Th	4 41	5.9	5 03	6.1	11 01	1.9	11 28	1.9
16	F	5 24	6.1	5 41	6.2	11 40	1.7	** **	***
17	Sa ●	6 02	6.2	6 17	6.4	00 06	1.7	12 16	1.6
18	Su	6 36	6.3	6 50	6.5	00 41	1.4	12 50	1.4
19	M	7 12	6.3	7 26	6.6	1 16	1.3	1 26	1.3
20	Tu	7 48	6.4	8 01	6.6	1 51	1.3	2 01	1.3
21	W	8 23	6.3	8 38	6.5	2 27	1.3	2 39	1.3
22	Th	9 00	6.3	9 16	6.4	3 05	1.3	3 18	1.4
23	F	9 40	6.2	9 58	6.3	3 43	1.4	3 58	1.7
24	Sa	10 24	6.0	10 46	6.2	4 26	1.7	4 43	1.8
25	Su	11 15	5.9	11 42	6.0	5 48	1.9	5 37	2.1
26	M	** **	***	12 19	5.7	6 14	2.1	6 47	2.2
27	Tu	00 52	5.8	1 35	5.7	7 30	2.2	8 06	2.2
28	W	2 09	5.8	2 50	5.9	8 49	2.1	9 23	2.0
29	Th	3 23	6.0	3 57	6.2	9 59	1.8	10 30	1.6
30	F	4 29	6.3	4 57	6.6	10 59	1.4	11 28	1.1
31	Sa ○	5 27	6.6	5 50	7.0	11 51	1.0	** **	***

AUGUST 2004

Adjusted for G.M.T. and British Summer Time. Height in meters (1 metre = 3ft)

DATE	DAY	HIGH WATER Morning Time	Ht m	Afternoon Time	Ht m	LOW WATER Morning Time	Ht m	Afternoon Time	Ht m
1	Su	6 18	6.8	6 38	7.2	00 19	0.6	12 40	0.7
2	M	7 04	6.9	7 25	7.3	1 08	0.4	1 27	0.5
3	Tu	7 50	6.9	8 09	7.2	1 56	0.4	2 12	0.6
4	W	8 32	6.8	8 52	7.0	2 40	0.5	2 55	0.7
5	Th	9 12	6.5	9 33	6.7	3 21	0.8	3 34	1.0
6	F	9 51	6.2	10 14	6.2	4 00	1.1	4 14	1.4
7	Sa	10 31	5.9	10 57	5.9	4 39	1.7	4 55	1.9
8	Su	11 16	5.5	11 47	5.5	5 22	2.1	5 42	2.3
9	M	** **	***	12 15	5.2	6 14	2.4	6 50	2.6
10	Tu	00 56	5.2	1 37	5.1	7 27	2.7	8 15	2.7
11	W	2 19	5.1	2 59	5.2	8 49	2.6	9 34	2.5
12	Th	3 32	5.3	4 01	5.6	9 54	2.4	10 30	2.2
13	F	4 26	5.6	4 46	6.0	10 44	2.0	11 13	1.8
14	Sa	5 09	6.0	5 25	6.2	11 24	1.7	11 50	1.4
15	Su	5 46	6.2	6 00	6.4	11 59	1.3	** **	***
16	M ●	6 19	6.4	6 32	6.6	00 24	1.2	12 33	1.1
17	Tu	6 51	6.5	7 06	6.8	00 56	1.0	1 06	0.9
18	W	7 25	6.6	7 40	6.8	1 30	0.9	1 40	0.8
19	Th	8 00	6.6	8 14	6.8	2 04	0.8	2 16	0.8
20	F	8 35	6.6	8 50	6.7	2 40	0.9	2 53	1.0
21	Sa	9 11	6.4	9 29	6.5	3 17	1.0	3 30	1.2
22	Su	9 52	6.2	10 13	6.2	3 54	1.3	4 11	1.6
23	M	10 40	5.9	11 08	5.8	4 38	1.8	5 03	2.0
24	Tu	11 44	5.6	** **	***	5 36	2.2	6 14	2.3
25	W	00 23	5.5	1 13	5.4	7 04	2.4	7 54	2.4
26	Th	1 57	5.4	2 43	5.6	8 43	2.3	9 23	2.1
27	F	3 25	5.7	3 57	6.1	9 58	1.9	10 31	1.4
28	Sa	4 31	6.2	4 53	6.6	10 56	1.3	11 25	0.9
29	Su	5 22	6.6	5 41	7.0	11 45	0.9	** **	***
30	M ○	6 06	6.9	6 24	7.3	00 10	0.5	12 28	0.6
31	Tu	6 46	7.1	7 04	7.4	00 52	0.3	1 07	0.4

neap range = 2.4m

spring range = 6m

Extracts from a tide table

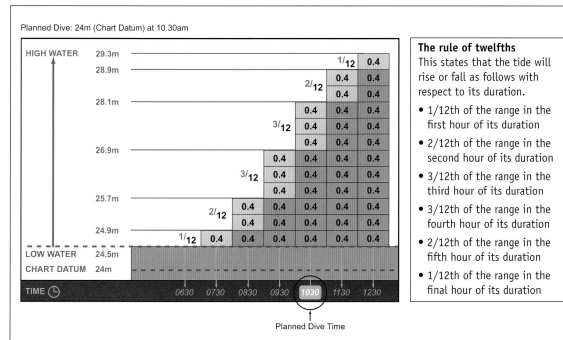

Planned Dive: 24m (Chart Datum) at 10.30am

Planned Dive Time

The rule of twelfths
This states that the tide will rise or fall as follows with respect to its duration.

- 1/12th of the range in the first hour of its duration
- 2/12th of the range in the second hour of its duration
- 3/12th of the range in the third hour of its duration
- 3/12th of the range in the fourth hour of its duration
- 2/12th of the range in the fifth hour of its duration
- 1/12th of the range in the final hour of its duration

Example: Using the rule of twelfths

We want to dive at a site of 24 metres charted depth, where low water is at 06.30h and the height is 0.5 m and high water is at 12.45h and the height is 5.3 m. Dive time is planned to be at 1030h. At low water the actual depth will be 24 m plus 0.5 m, which is 24.5 m. At high water the depth will be 24 m plus 5.3 m. The tidal range will be 5.3 m minus 0.5 m, which is 4.8 m. The rule of twelfths tells us that:

- in the first hour after low water the tide will rise by 1/12th of the range or 1/12 x 4.8 m = 0.4 m
  depth on site will be 24.5 m + 0.4 = 24.9 m
- in the second hour the tide will rise by two more 1/12ths
  depth on site will be 24.5 m + 0.4 +0.8 = 25.7 m
- in the third hour the tide will rise by three more 1/12ths
  depth on site will be 24.5 m + 0.4 + 0.8 + 1.2 = 26.9 m
- in the fourth hour the tide will rise by three more 1/12ths
  depth on site will be 24.5 m + 0.4 + 0.8 + 1.2 + 1.2 = 28.1 m
- in the fifth hour the tide will rise by two more 1/12ths
  depth on site will be 24.5 m + 0.4 + 0.8 + 1.2 + 1.2 + 0.8 = 28.9 m
- in the sixth hour the tide will rise by a final 1/12th
  depth on site will be 24.5 m + 0.4 + 0.8 + 1.2 + 1.2 + 0.8 + 0.4 = 29.3 m

So, at 10.30h, four hours after low water the depth will be 28.1 m. This could be calculated more quickly by saying the number of twelfths that the water will rise by in four hours is 1/12 + 2/12 + 3/12 + 3/12 = 9/12ths. Then you add 9/12ths of the range to the height at low water.
The same procedure can be used to calculate the depth of water for a dive between high and low water.

Local tidal anomalies

Tidal curves, given in almanacs, are another method of predicting the height of the tide. They take into account any local tidal anomalies and are, therefore, more accurate than the rule of twelfths. Because they are specific to a location you must use the curve for the nearest standard port to the dive site. When using information from the Admiralty Tide Tables remember that times are given in universal time (UT) – you must correct for any local time differences. In the UK you will need to add one hour to UT to correct for British Summer Time (BST) when it is in operation. Tide tables from other sources may or may not use UT, however they will be clearly marked.

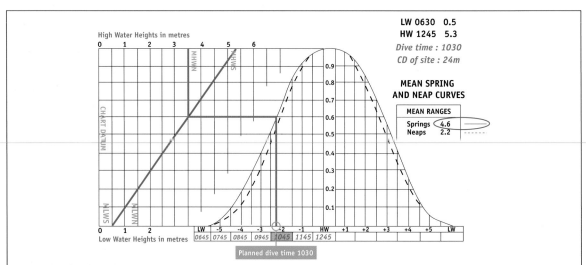

Example 2: Using tidal curves

As in the previous example, we want to dive at a site of 24 metres charted depth, where low water is at 06.30 h and the height is 0.5 m and high water is at 12.45 h and the height is 5.3 m. Dive time is planned to be 10.30 h.

The tidal range is 5.3 - 0.5 m = 4.8 m and, referring to the mean ranges box on the diagram tells us that this range indicates a spring tide. This means that the tidal curve shown as an unbroken line should be used as a reference. If it were a neap tide you would use the broken line on the tidal curve diagram.

- Enter the HW time and hourly increments to 10.30 h (planned dive time) into the bottom row of boxes beneath the curve diagram.
- On the left hand side, draw a line from the bottom line marked LW, for the depth obtained from the tide tables, 0.5 m, to the top line marked HW to the depth obtained from the tide tables, 5.3 m. This is the tidal range line.
- Draw a line vertically until it reaches the unbroken spring tidal curve which is 2.15 h before high water.
- Draw a horizontal line starting where this vertical line meets the tidal curve and finishing on the tidal range line.
- Use this intersection with the tidal range line to read off depth expected at 10.30 h, by drawing a vertical line from the intersection up to the depth scale.
- The depth expected at 10.30 h is about 3.5 m. So the depth above chart datum will be 24 m + 3.5 m = 27.5 m.
- If you are planning a dive after high water, you can use the other half of the curve in the same way to calculate expected water depth.

Tidal streams

The movement of water associated with the tide gives rise to tidal streams, which flow in different directions according to the state of the tide locally. Navigators need to allow for the effects on the boat of tidal streams when planning a passage and divers are interested in their effects on a dive site. Some sites are best dived at slack water, when the water is moving as little as possible. Others, such as drift dives, require a manageable current. Tidal streams are described by stating the three-figure notation of the direction in which the current is flowing, unlike winds where the opposite system is used. So a current flowing from east to west would be shown with a direction of 270 degrees.

Tidal flow information can be found in a tidal stream table on a chart. The table contains predicted speed in knots, for both springs (Sp) and neaps (Np), and direction of the current at hourly intervals for six hours either side of high water at a standard port. Purple tidal diamond symbols, containing a code letter, are found on the chart. Each diamond corresponds to a column of data in the table, taken from measurements made at that place on the chart, marked by the same code letter.

You will need to confirm the time of high water for the day in question using a tide table. Then you can find the speed and direction of the current at any time of the day. On spring tides the currents are faster than on neap tides.

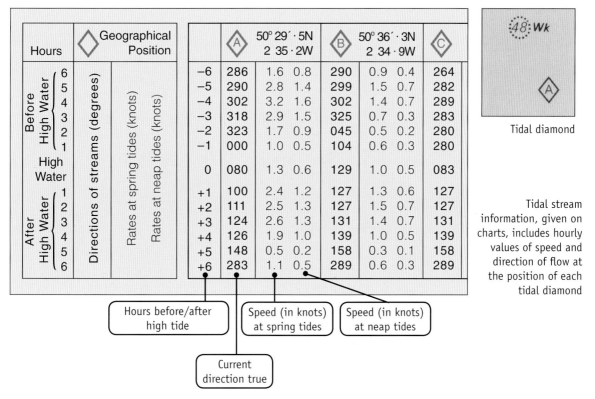

Hours		Geographical Position				A 50° 29´·5N 2 35·2W			B 50° 36´·3N 2 34·9W			C
Before High Water	6	Directions of streams (degrees)	Rates at spring tides (knots)	Rates at neap tides (knots)	−6	286	1.6	0.8	290	0.9	0.4	264
	5				−5	290	2.8	1.4	299	1.5	0.7	282
	4				−4	302	3.2	1.6	302	1.4	0.7	289
	3				−3	318	2.9	1.5	325	0.7	0.3	283
	2				−2	323	1.7	0.9	045	0.5	0.2	280
	1				−1	000	1.0	0.5	104	0.6	0.3	280
High Water					0	080	1.3	0.6	129	1.0	0.5	083
After High Water	1				+1	100	2.4	1.2	127	1.3	0.6	127
	2				+2	111	2.5	1.3	127	1.5	0.7	127
	3				+3	124	2.6	1.3	131	1.4	0.7	131
	4				+4	126	1.9	1.0	139	1.0	0.5	139
	5				+5	148	0.5	0.2	158	0.3	0.1	158
	6				+6	283	1.1	0.5	289	0.6	0.3	289

Hours before/after high tide

Speed (in knots) at spring tides

Speed (in knots) at neap tides

Current direction true

Tidal diamond

Tidal stream information, given on charts, includes hourly values of speed and direction of flow at the position of each tidal diamond

Tidal stream atlas

Time is relative to high water at a standard port. You will have to apply the correction given in the almanac to calculate time on site.

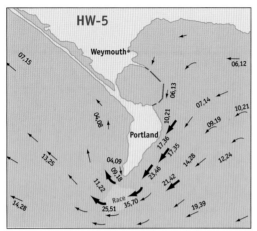

5 hours before HW Plymouth (Devonport)

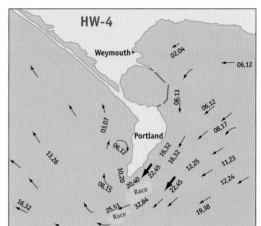

4 hours before HW Plymouth (Devonport)

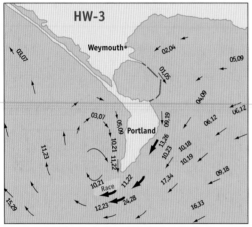

3 hours before HW Plymouth (Devonport)

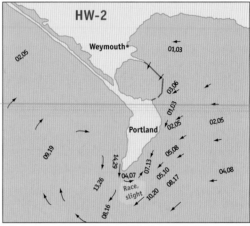

2 hours before HW Plymouth (Devonport)

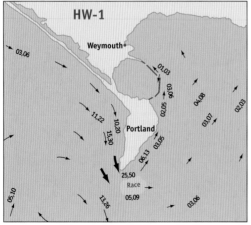

1 hour before HW Plymouth (Devonport)

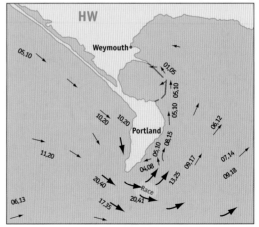

HW Plymouth (Devonport)

Speed is given in knots, neap followed by spring. 06 = 0.6 knot, 11 = 1.1 knot.

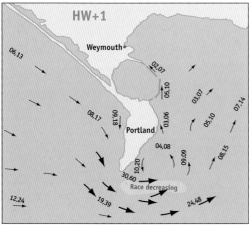

1 hour after HW Plymouth (Devonport)

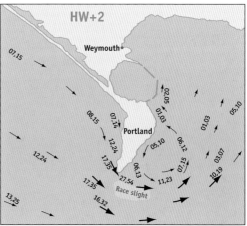

2 hours after HW Plymouth (Devonport)

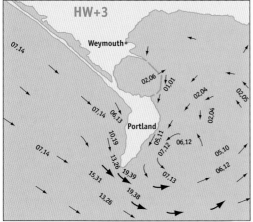

3 hours after HW Plymouth (Devonport)

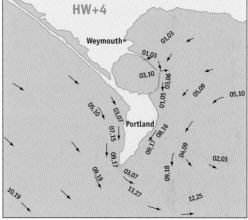

4 hours after HW Plymouth (Devonport)

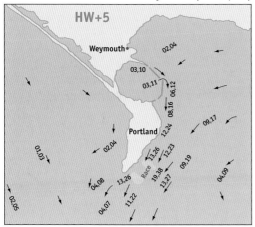

5 hours after HW Plymouth (Devonport)

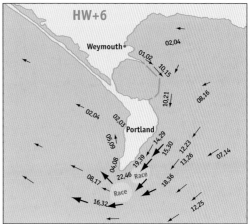

6 hours after HW Plymouth (Devonport)

Local currents

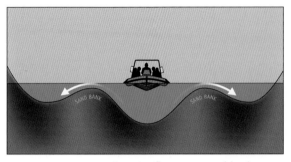

As water flows over sand banks cross currents are formed

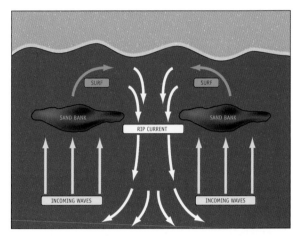

Rip currents flow out to sea – to escape them, move parallel to the shore until you reach calm waters

Turbulent water

There may be other factors that contribute to the tidal streams and the height of the tide on any particular day. Strong winds, for example, can have very marked effects. Wind blowing against the tide can happen anywhere and will cause worsening surface conditions. The topography of the sea bed is an important factor in determining the way the water flows. Local knowledge is invaluable when deciding when to dive at a site with complex tidal streams.

There are two chart symbols that show disturbed water: one for overfalls and tide rips and one for eddies. The waves in such areas can be surprisingly large. If there is another route available to you that avoids the rough water it would be prudent to take it.

In calm surface conditions, you may sometimes see a roughening of the water, or a break in the surface pattern. This is a tide rip, caused by the meeting of tidal streams that run in opposing directions.

Sometimes depth and the configuration of the sea bed, combined with strong localised tidal streams or eddies, create local conditions known as overfalls. These can often be seen as breaking waves caused by a strong tidal stream crossing rapidly shoaling waters, an irregular bottom or an underwater obstruction.

In confined waters, such as estuaries and harbours, there is a possibility of strong cross currents. For example, in a narrow channel with sand or mud banks lying parallel to the shore the flood tide will reach the top of the banks and will start to fill the inner channel. At this point a surface tidal stream will form which will cause your boat to be drawn towards the shallow water.

Rip currents

Rip currents occur when water is driven over a sand bar or reef by the flood tide or by adverse weather conditions. The water is then funnelled back through narrow openings in the sand bar or reef, causing a very strong back current. If you are caught in a rip current, you should move parallel to the shore until you are clear of it, rather than try to move against it.

Check the weather forecast before putting to sea

Weather

Weather forecasting is a vital part of any plan for a diving trip in a small boat, especially in areas of the world that have variable weather such as the UK. The weather conditions that are of greatest concern to divers are wind and poor surface visibility caused by sea fog or precipitation of some kind. These can affect the underwater conditions as well as the surface sea state. There are several useful sources of weather forecasts, but you must be able to understand the processes behind the weather in order to get the most out of the information given in forecasts.

Talking about the weather

Weather – daily conditions

Climate – weather described over a long period (of decades or more)

Precipitation – rain, sleet, snow etc

Prevailing wind – the most common direction from which the wind blows

Veer – wind changes direction clockwise eg S to SW

Back – wind changes direction anti-clockwise eg N to NW

Air temperatures

What makes weather?

The sun warms the planet's surface and this creates high and low pressure bands around Earth, which govern our overall weather patterns.

The high-altitude winds that blow around our planet cause secondary areas of high and low pressure to be created in different places on Earth's surface, which also contribute to the irregular day-to-day movements of air that give us both climate and weather.

High-pressure centres or anticyclones form when cooled air falls back to Earth. Winds will move out from high-pressure centres to areas of lower pressure.

Low-pressure centres or depressions form when warm air rises up from the Earth. Winds will move into low-pressure centres from areas of higher pressure.

The Coriolis effect, which is a result of the rotation of the Earth, means that in the northern hemisphere winds spiral clockwise out of high-pressure centres and anti-clockwise into low-pressure centres. In the southern hemisphere the effect is reversed.

How convection works

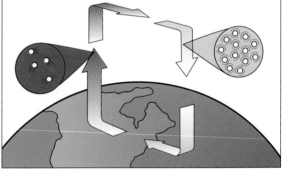

Warm air expands
Particles move rapidly
Air is less dense
Pressure decreases so air continues to rise

Cool air contracts
Particles slow down
Air is more dense
Pressure increases so air continues to fall

The Earth's surface is mainly heated by solar radiation which causes convection currents to be set up

Air temperatures

As the Earth moves around the sun, it rotates on its tilted axis so that during the cycle of a year some areas get more sun than others. Also, different surfaces on Earth absorb different amounts of sunlight and therefore heat up at different rates. For example, bare soil and sand absorb more of the sun's radiation than ice or snow do. The variations in temperature experienced by an area generate its seasons. Near the equator, there is not much seasonal variation in temperature, but the further away from the equator you move the greater the seasonal temperature changes are.

The atmosphere is the thin layer of life-supporting gases that surrounds the Earth. It is in the atmosphere that the weather is created. When the surface of the Earth is warm, the air above is heated. The warm air expands, becomes less dense and a bubble of warm air begins to rise. Rising currents of warm air like this are known as thermals.

As the warm air continues to rise away from the warm surface of the Earth, it begins to cool. The air becomes denser and begins to sink towards the surface again. When it hits the surface, the dense, cooled air, which is at a higher pressure than its surroundings, will move towards any areas of lower pressure, such as those where the pressure is reduced by warmed air rising. This circulation of warm and cold air currents is called convection, and it happens on a large and small scale all over the Earth's surface.

Rising air leaves behind a low-pressure centre. Cooled air falling back towards the surface creates a high-pressure centre and the air moves horizontally from high to low-pressure areas to create wind.

The rotation of the Earth has an effect on the atmosphere known as the Coriolis effect, which deflects winds from the obvious direct path between high and low-pressure areas. In the northern hemisphere, this causes the winds to spiral clockwise out of high-pressure areas and anticlockwise into low-pressure areas. Weather forecasters call high-pressure centres anticyclones. Low-pressure centres are called cyclones or depressions.

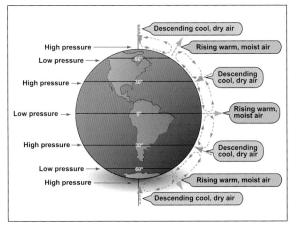

There is a pattern of high and low-pressure bands around the world

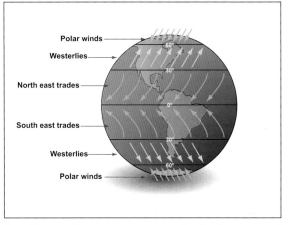

Prevailing weather systems are generated by the movement of air from high to low-pressure areas

Air pressure

Around the world there are areas where high or low-pressure areas predominate. At the equator the effect of a constantly high amount of sunshine or solar radiation is to warm the air which rises and creates a band of low pressure. As this equatorial air rises, it cools and falls back to the surface at latitudes of 30 degrees both north and south of the equator. Here it creates high-pressure bands. The high-pressure air then moves out towards low-pressure areas found at latitudes of 60 degrees to the north in the northern hemisphere and to the south in the southern hemisphere. As the air fills the low-pressure areas it is heated again by the Earth's surface and begins to rise, maintaining the low-pressure bands at 60 degrees. Some air will move back towards to the equator, some will meet cold, high-pressure air moving down from the poles. The cold air lifts the warmer air, which cools and sinks down onto the pole to maintain the polar high-pressure areas.

The air moving from high to low-pressure areas tries to take the most direct route. But the Coriolis effect, deflects these winds sideways. In the northern hemisphere they are deflected to the right, in the southern hemisphere they are deflected to the left.

The direction of the winds blowing from high to low-pressure areas gives us the prevailing wind in those areas, although other influences may affect wind strength and direction some of the time. The names given to the prevailing winds date back to sailing days when vessels were dependent on the winds to sail around the world.

The main high and low-pressure bands around the Earth determine the overall weather patterns. But very high-altitude winds blowing around the Earth in the direction of its spin also have an effect on the system, contributing to everyday variations in the weather through their effects on the formation and movement of high and low pressure areas. The strongest, known as the jet streams, are at 60 degrees north and south, where the cool polar air meets warmer air. Weaker high-level winds exist at 30 degrees north and south. These high-level winds follow wavy paths around Earth and move the surface lows and highs around. As a result, air patterns can become disrupted so that lows form in high-pressure areas and highs in low-pressure areas.

Weather forecasters often show maps created from pressure readings of an area. On such maps, places of equal pressure are joined by lines called isobars. Where isobars are spread out, the pressure gradient is shallow and the winds will be light. Where isobars are packed together, the pressure gradient is steeper and winds stronger. Although there is a notion of average atmospheric pressure, which has been set at 1013 millibars, areas of high and low pressure on weather maps are defined in relation to the

Weather fronts

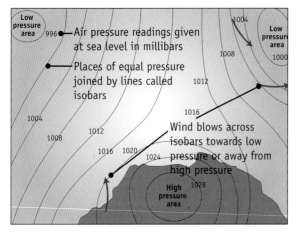

An example of a pressure map

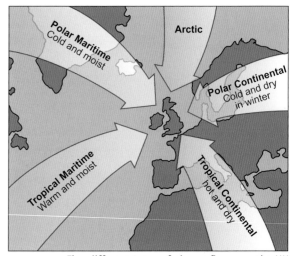

Five different types of air can flow over the UK

pressure in the areas surrounding them because this is what affects their behaviour. For example 1004 mb may be termed low pressure if surrounded by air at 1028 mb or high pressure if surrounded by air at 994 mb.

Weather fronts

Air masses originating in different parts of the world have different characteristics. And they keep those characteristics as they move around the world. Air arriving from the tropics will be warm and moist. Air that has travelled across land may be cold and dry. Where air masses meet they form a boundary called a front. They push against each other at the front and depending on their characteristics, one of several things can happen.

In both hemispheres the main fronts are the polar fronts. In the northern hemisphere, cold polar air meets warmer tropical air at the polar front. In some places, warm air can push into the cold polar air, or cold air can push into the warmer air. These bulges occur because the pressure along the front is uneven.

In these bulges along the polar front, the warm air can rise above the cool air, creating areas of low pressure called frontal depressions. The surrounding air, both warm and cold, then spirals into these depressions, along the pressure gradient, and creates wind. This air movement brings different types of air together and this is how warm

or cold fronts develop.

A cold front is where a cool air mass moves into an area of warmer air. It pushes under the warm air and forces it to rise. As the warm air rises it cools and is forced to give up its water vapour, which forms thick clouds. A cold front is shown on a weather map as a line marked with triangles.

A warm front is where warm air moves into an area of colder air. Along the front the warm air will rise over the colder air and clouds will form. Warm fronts are shown on a weather map as a line marked with semicircles.

Cold fronts move faster than warm fronts and will eventually catch up with a warm front to form an occluded front, which is shown on a weather map as a line marked with alternate triangles and semicircles.

This process may be speeded up by the Earth's high-level winds in some places. Also the greater the temperature difference between the warm and cold air the faster the warm air will rise and the quicker the depression will form. This will create stronger winds.

Frontal depressions generally produce unsettled weather, which is not good news for diving at sea. By keeping an eye on the actual weather you can watch the weather system pass and determine whether or not the forecast was accurate. If not, you will be able to take account of the new situation, based on your observations.

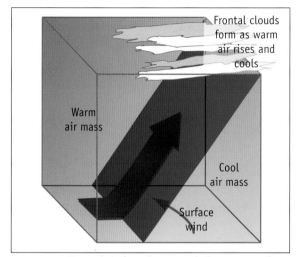

Warm air is forced over cool air at a warm front

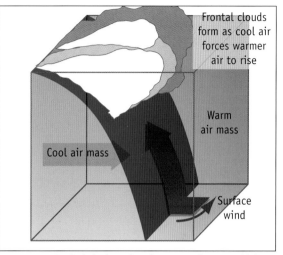

Cool air is forced under warm air at a cold front

The position of the polar front changes with the seasons: in the northern hemisphere, in the summer, the polar front usually moves north of the British Isles and depressions pass to the north of us. If however the polar front does not make it that far, we will have poor, unsettled summer weather as depressions continue to hit us.

Low-pressure systems

What sort of weather is associated with a depression approaching and passing over us? Unfortunately depressions generally come close together and bring periods of unsettled weather.

The first signs of an approaching warm front are the high-level streaky clouds called cirrus, sometimes also called mare's tails. Because they form high up in the atmosphere, cirrus clouds are blown a long way in front of the approaching front by the high-level winds. In the UK they usually approach from the west or south-west.

As the warm front gets closer, the high-level cloud may become more uniform, though there is still only a thin layer. This is called cirro-stratus cloud. You may see the effect of this thin cloud layer as a halo around the sun. Eventually a blanket layer of stratus cloud appears, and cloud base gets lower. This will be accompanied by rain, slight and intermittent at first but gradually getting

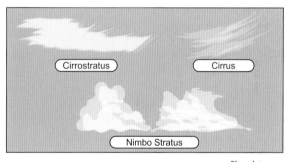

Cloud types

heavier and more persistent. Barometric pressure will fall and the winds will increase in speed. Wind direction will back from west or south-west to south or south-east as the front approaches.

As the front passes there may be a heavier period of rain, and then the pressure will begin to rise, the rain will ease and the wind direction will veer into the west again. Depressions move at different speeds and the rain associated with a warm front can take from six to 24 hours to pass. In the warm sector, behind the warm front, surface visibility can be poor, due to showers and low cloud. If the sea is cold there may well be sea fog. The wind remains fairly steady in speed and direction,

High pressure sytems

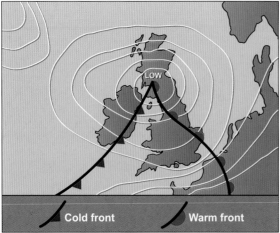
A typical frontal depression system

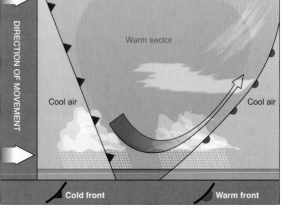
A cross-section through a typical depression

typically to the south or west. The pressure will remain steady and the temperature will rise.

The cold front is usually a much more sudden transition than the warm front. As the cloud thickens and lowers, large cumulus and/or nimbus clouds will appear. These give heavy, perhaps thundery, showers. You will typically see a fall in pressure and the wind will back a little from west-south-west to south-west and increase in strength, especially before and during rain showers. The cold front passes quickly and behind it the pressure will rise and temperature will fall, but the wind may still be strong and gusty. The most noticeable change will be in the surface visibility, which will improve greatly after the front. The weather will remain showery with broken cloud.

The usual sequence of events in a westerly pattern of weather, such as in the UK, is a warm front, warm sector, cold front, followed by cold air and showers, then a brief spell of fine weather followed by the next series of fronts. If the low is occluded then the warm sector will be missing and you will see the warm front cloud and rain followed by the cold front cloud and rain.

High-pressure systems

The frontal sequence can be interrupted by the development of a blocking high, so called because they block the usual west to east flow of weather systems. These are often very stable, static or near static features that can turn even large, low pressure systems away. They produce long periods of stable, settled weather.

Anticyclones, or high-pressure systems, are not dynamic like lows, but they can cause some subtle changes in the weather. In predominantly maritime areas such as the UK, the air circulating around a high has had substantial time over the ocean and the low-level air will be quite moist. Low cloud will form wherever there is enough turbulent mixing to raise the air high enough for condensation to occur. It may also be quite foggy. The North Sea is well known for its 'sea fret' or advection fog. This is caused by a warm stream of air blowing over a cool sea, from the east in the case of the North Sea. Rapid condensation gives rise to the sea fog, which can arrive very rapidly and will reduce the surface visibility to almost zero.

Sea breezes

If the weather has been good for several days, sea breezes may occur. Air warmed by the heating of the land will rise and leave a local area of low pressure. Cooler air is drawn in off the sea to equalise the pressure. As the warmed air rises, it will cool and drop back down over the sea. Quite often, these onshore sea breezes pick up during the afternoon. Depending on the direction of any existing wind, they can appear to strengthen an onshore wind, or

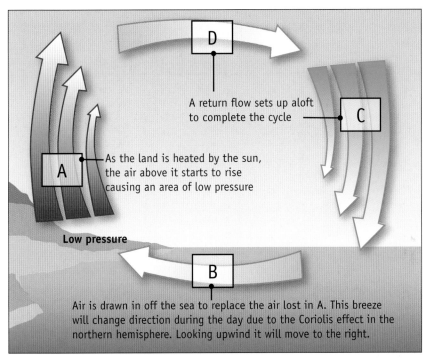

A return flow sets up aloft
to complete the cycle

As the land is heated by the sun,
the air above it starts to rise
causing an area of low pressure

Low pressure

Air is drawn in off the sea to replace the air lost in A. This breeze
will change direction during the day due to the Coriolis effect in the
northern hemisphere. Looking upwind it will move to the right.

Sea breezes can form on all coasts during high-pressure systems

still or reverse an offshore wind. A sea breeze alone, in the absence of any background wind, can be strong enough to make diving conditions difficult.

At night, the land cools rapidly but the sea loses heat more slowly and will be warmer than the land. The air above the sea will rise and create an area of low pressure. Cooler land air will move in to equalise the pressure. The rising air will cool and drop back down towards the land. The resulting offshore wind may smooth the sea close to shore.

A much shorter-lived weather phenomenon, but one that usually brings a day or two of fine weather is a high-pressure ridge, which will often be sandwiched between two depressions.

Weather forecasts

Making any type of forecast is difficult and the weather is no exception to that, particularly in areas such as the UK, which is in a fairly active weather zone on the edge of a large continent. In order to make the best use of the forecast, it is important to monitor actual conditions. This will give you an idea of where you are in the weather system described in the forecast. Weather systems do not always arrive with their forecast speed or intensity.

Observation of wind speed and direction and cloud cover, combined with the latest forecast, will tell you a great deal about the next few hours at least. A useful law to remember is Buys-Ballot's law which states that: if in the northern hemisphere you stand with your back to the wind, the pressure will be lower on your left hand than your right. The reverse is true in the southern hemisphere. This will help you position yourself within the weather system. It may be, for example, that a low has passed to the north of you rather than the south and this would have an effect on the local wind direction.

In the northern hemisphere, if a low is passing to the north of you, you can expect southerly winds, followed

Buys Ballots law

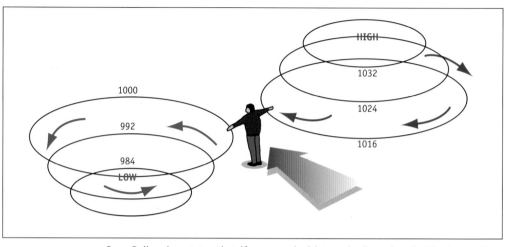

Buys Ballots law states that if you stand with your back to the wind in the northern hemisphere, LOW pressure will be on your left and HIGH pressure will be on your right

by westerlies and then northerlies. If a low is passing to the south of you, you can expect southerly winds, followed by easterlies and then northerlies. This could make a difference to your day's diving.

A land forecast with a synoptic chart, together with an inshore waters forecast, or other appropriate marine forecast, should give you enough information. Weather forecasts use particular terminology to make them both precise and brief and you will need to be familiar with the terms used (see *Weather forecast terminology*, page 158).

The UK shipping forecast is broadcast daily on BBC Radio 4 at 00.48h (LW, MW, FM), 05.35h (LW, MW, FM), 12.01h (LW only) and 17.54h (LW only), except on Saturdays when the second forecast of the day is delayed until 05.56h. A summary of gale warnings is followed by a general synopsis of the weather for the next 24 hours and any expected changes in that time. Then forecasts for each sea area are given. They are valid for the next 24 hours, they give wind direction and speed, weather and visibility. It is best to make a note of the shipping forecast

for the area that you are interested in, as it is all read rather quickly. However, sea areas are large and variation close to land does occur, so sea-area forecast are not always useful for small boats staying relatively close to shore. For this reason there is also an inshore waters forecast.

Both the 00.48h and the 05.35h forecast also include weather reports from coastal stations. These take the form of wind direction and force, present weather, visibility, sea level pressure and tendency. A forecast for inshore waters, up to 12 miles offshore, is broadcast after the 00.48h and 05.35h reports from coastal stations. This gives a forecast of wind, weather and visibility followed by reports from selected coastal stations.

Gale warnings are broadcast at the earliest opportunity after receipt, as well as after the next news bulletin. Sea area Trafalgar appears only in the 00.48h forecast. The coastguard local to a site will also give you local weather information, such as the area and inshore forecasts, by either telephone or VHF radio.

The Beaufort wind scale				
Force	Wind speed (knots)	Description	Sea state	Probable wave height (m)
0	0-1	calm	like a mirror	0
1	1-3	light air	ripples like scales are formed	0
2	4-6	light breeze	small wavelets, still short but more pronounced, not breaking	0.1
3	7-10	gentle breeze	Large wavelets, crests begin to break, a few white horses	0.4
4	11-16	moderate breeze	small waves growing longer, fairly frequent white horses	1
5	17-21	fresh breeze	moderate waves, taking more pronounced form, many white horses, perhaps some spray	2
6	22-27	strong breeze	large waves forming, white-foam crests more extensive, probably some spray	3
7	28-33	near gale	sea heaps up, white foam from breaking waves begins to blow in streaks	4
8	34-40	gale	moderately high waves of greater length, edge of crests break into spindrift, foam blown in well marked streaks	5.5
9	41-47	severe gale	high waves with tumbling crests, dense streaks of foam, spray may affect visibility	7
10	48-55	storm	very high waves with long overhanging crests, dense streams of foam make surface of sea white. Heavy tumbling sea. Visibility affected	9
11	56-63	violent storm	exceptionally high waves, sea completely covered with long white patches of foam; edges of wave crests blown into froth. Visibility affected	11
12	64-plus	hurricane	air filled with foam and spray, sea completely white with driving spray, visbility very seriously affected	14

Note: the sea state and probable wave heights are a guide to what may be expected in the open sea. In enclosed waters, or near land with an offshore wind, wave heights will be less, but possibly steeper - particularly with wind against tide.

Marine forecasts

Marine weather forecast terminology	
Timing	
Imminent	within 6 hours of the forecast
Soon	between 6 and 12 hours after the forecast
Later	between 12 and 24 hours after the forecast
Visibility	
Good	more than 5 nautical miles
Moderate	between 2 to 5 nautical miles
Poor	1,000 metres to 2 nautical miles
Fog	less than 1,000 metres
Speed of movement of pressure systems	
Slowly	up to 15 knots
Steadily	between 15 and 25 knots
Rather quickly	between 25 and 35 knots
Rapidly	between 35 and 45 knots
Very rapidly	more than 45 knots
Wind direction	
Veering	the changing of the wind in a clockwise direction, that is SW to W
Backing	the changing of the wind in an anticlockwise direction, that is W to SW
Becoming cyclonic	indicates considerable change in wind direction across the path of a depression

Land forecasts are broadcast at various times on BBC Radio Four and on television. They may include an outlook period up to 48 hours beyond the shipping forecast. Television or newspaper synoptic charts can give much information. The lines drawn on the charts are isobars, joining places of equal barometric pressure. Pressures are given in millibars. The closer together the isobars are, the stronger the wind will be. Land forecasts give wind speed and direction and an indication of the prevailing weather conditions.

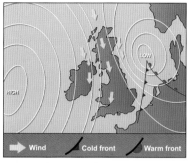

Wind | Cold front | Warm front

A depression has moved out into the North Sea and high-pressure is forming to the west. The isobars show an area of strong, northerly gales where the two systems meet.

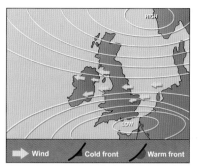

Wind | Cold front | Warm front

A depression has formed over France and an anticyclone, or high, has formed over Scandinavia. The eastern coast of England will experience very strong easterly winds, which will have the whole area of the North Sea over which to generate large waves.

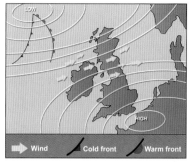

Wind | Cold front | Warm front

A depression over Iceland combined with an anticyclone over France will result in a very strong, westerly winds. The west coast of the UK will have strong onshore winds. The west coast will be rough because the Atlantic Ocean is generating a considerable ground swell, which travels much further than the storms that cause it.

There are certain patterns of weather that bring strong winds to UK shores and that means difficult boating and diving conditions at sea. The isobar charts (above) will help you to recognise such situations when they occur in land-based weather forecasts

Land area forecasts use different terminology	
Wind strength	
Calm	Beaufort force 0
Light	1 to 3
Moderate	4
Fresh	5
Strong	6 to 7
Gale	8 and above
Visibility	
Mist	1,000 to 2,000 metres
Fog	less than 1,000 metres
Dense fog	less than 50 metres

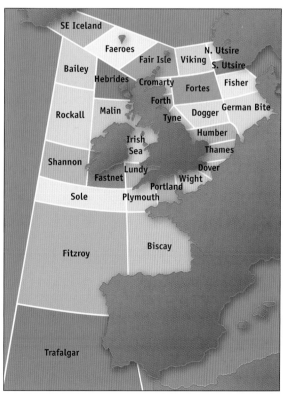

UK shipping forecast areas

Chapter seven

Using charter boats

To dive on hard-to-reach sites or in exotic locations often means chartering a hard boat with a skipper and crew. Dive boat skippers have a wealth of local knowledge and experience to support the dive marshal and the diving group. It is tempting to leave everything to the skipper except for the diving, but a club dive marshal should still go through the planning and risk-assessment procedure as preparation for liaising with the skipper on the day.

Dive boats suitable for day charters vary in size but they generally carry ten to twelve divers. They are usually highly manoeuvrable boats with a small cabin that offers some protection from the weather and somewhere to store a dry bag. There should be plenty of kitting-up space on deck, but personal diving equipment should be stored in bags to help keep space clear.

Entry to the water is usually either by rolling off the side or a stride entry over, or through a purpose-built gap in the gunwale. There will be a ladder or lift to get back into the boat. Other facilities may include a kettle to make hot drinks, and a head (toilet). These boats generally stay away from port all day.

Larger hard boats that are used for longer charters could be described as floating hotels, offering a diving, catering and accommodation package. Such 'liveaboards' have cabins, showers, heads, a saloon and a galley (kitchen). And, of course, a compressor for filling diving cylinders. Larger boats may also have a longer cruising range, often travelling further afield to remote, infrequently dived sites. They are less manoeuvrable than day boats, but may have their own tender to ferry divers to the entry point of a dive and to pick them up at the end. Liveaboards come in a variety of shapes and sizes. In the UK there are still a number of converted fishing vessels in use as charter boats. Purpose-built dive boats tend to predominate overseas.

Legislation

Different designs of boat suit different purposes and it is worth considering all the needs of your group when you are choosing a charter boat. Vessels with a narrow beam and well-flared bows are built for speed. On the other hand, a chunkier profile may provide more comfortable accommodation.

You should expect any charter vessel to be equipped with a high standard of electronic navigation aids. Essential items are radar, GPS, an echo sounder, VHF radio, and maybe a satellite phone.

Legislation governing commercial vessels

If you undertake the commercial hire of a charter vessel for a diving trip you should make sure that the vessel complies with the appropriate government safety legislation. This will ensure the standard of the boat, the crew, its fittings, and its emergency equipment. Without certification, an operator can get away with being poorly equipped and risks being prosecuted for non-compliance.

International treaties govern the various areas of a commercial vessel's operations. The International Convention on Safety of Life at Sea (SOLAS) is implemented in UK legislation by the Merchant Shipping Regulations (MSRs). All Merchant Shipping in UK waters must comply with these. For navigation, collision avoidance and pollution, any vessel, irrespective of size, must comply with The International Rules for the Prevention of Collisions at Sea and The International Convention for the Prevention of Pollution from Ships. These are also implemented in UK legislation by the MSRs.

However, vessels up to 24 metres load-line length and engaged at sea in activities on a commercial basis, carrying cargo or not more than 12 passengers, or providing a service in which neither cargo nor passengers are carried, can comply with the MCA's harmonised Small Commercial Vessel Code of Practice. This is seen by the UK's MCA as an acceptable alternative to the Merchant Shipping Regulations, which would otherwise apply.

Vessels operating at sea for commercial purposes are also required, under merchant shipping legislation, to have a valid load-line certificate. Again, certification within the MCA code of practice for small vessels provides a legal alternative to a UK Load-Line Certificate for vessels under 24 metres. Owners can opt to use the MSRs to obtain load-line certification, but complying with the code of practice, which is specifically designed for small commercial vessels, is more straightforward.

The code of practice relates to the construction of a vessel, its machinery, equipment and stability, and to the correct operation of a vessel so that safety standards are maintained. It also deals with manning a vessel and the qualifications needed for senior members of the crew.

A vessel may apply for an MCA Small Commercial Vessel Certificate allowing it to operate in one of six designated areas (see *Areas of operation of small commercial vessels*, page 163), and provisions under the code vary depending on the area of operation.

What to expect on a hard boat

Accommodation

On smaller day boats, the deck is usually kept clear to provide a large, working area for the crew and the divers. There may be very little shelter from the elements except in the wheelhouse, so the divers should be prepared to live outside for most of the day. It is essential to bring appropriate clothing – weatherproof or sunproof depending on the location – and food and drink for the day. A dry bag will protect your possessions on deck, and a sandwich box will protect your lunch.

It is worth checking with the skipper how they would like your equipment to be loaded and stowed. Every boat has a different layout that dictates where weightbelts, cylinders and kitbags should be stowed. If the dive marshal confirms the buddy pairs at this stage, then kit can be arranged in buddy pair order.

On larger liveaboards, the deck accommodation tends

Areas of Operation of Small Commercial Vessels

Category 6 to sea, within 3 miles from a nominated departure point(s) named in the certificate and never more then 3 miles from land, in favourable weather and daylight

Category 5 up to 20 miles from a nominated departure point named in the certificate, in favourable weather and daylight

Category 4 up to 20 miles from a safe haven, in favourable weather and daylight

Category 3 up to 20 miles from a safe haven

Category 2 up to 60 miles from a safe haven

Category 1 up to 150 miles from a safe haven

'Favourable weather' means wind, sea and visibility conditions that are deemed by the skipper to be safe for a small vessel to operate within the limits applied to it; or conditions existing throughout a voyage in which the effects, either individually or in combination, of swell, height of waves, strength of wind and visibility cause no hazard to the safety of the vessel, including handling ability.

'Safe haven' means a harbour or shelter of any kind that affords safe entry and protection form the force of the weather.

The MCA's harmonised Small Commercial Vessel Code of Practice is available on the MCA website www.mcga.gov.uk.

to be aft of the bridge. Usually a deckhouse will be fitted out as a saloon, with tables and chairs, and this will double up as the mess with the galley at one side.

Sleeping accommodation on larger vessels usually consists of bunks with storage lockers and sometimes hand basins and showers. Everything is designed to function in rough weather: shelves and bunks tend to have raised retaining edges and locker doors have secure catches. Loose kit should routinely be put away when not in use, otherwise it will all end up on the floor due to the boat's motion. Living accommodation may well be heated or air-conditioned, depending on the boat's location. A drying area for diving suits may also be provided.

Washing and toilet facilities on day boats tend to be basic. On larger vessels there is more space and facilities are generally better. Boat toilets, or 'heads', discharge either to a tank or to the sea, so there are various common sense rules to be aware of. It may be that you are requested not to use the facilities and discharge waste or washing water at the dive site or in harbour for example. There are usually local regulations governing this. The skipper, keen to avoid blockages, will no doubt give excellent instructions on the use of the facilities. It is possible to sink a boat by leaving the head-water inlet open and allowing sea water, usually used to flush the bowl, into the boat. If in doubt, ask.

Safety systems

Larger vessels will be divided into a number of compartments by watertight bulkheads. If such a vessel is holed, closing the bulkhead doors will isolate the problem and maintain the buoyancy of the rest of the boat, until help arrives. In the event of a fire or flood, you should find two escape routes from each compartment using companionways (stairs) of adequate dimensions.

Fire-fighting systems are most important, as fire aboard a vessel is one of the most life-threatening situations that can occur. Appropriate fire extinguishers will be located around the boat and there may well be an automated extinguisher system in the engine room. The skipper's safety briefing will include what to do in case of fire.

All boats accumulate water in the lowest part of their hull - the bilges. Hard boats have bilge pumps. These can be electrical or driven mechanically by the engine, with a manual option in case of engine failure.

Safety equipment – such as life rafts, first aid kits, sound-signalling equipment and distress flares – is a legal requirement of regulatory authorities around the world. Many charter boats carry first-aid oxygen for use in diving incidents. Check its whereabouts and familiarise yourself with its operation. Also check with the skipper the best method for retrieving an incapacitated or unconscious diver.

Liveaboards are likely to make frequent night passages and will have the required navigation lights and aids to navigation.

Working with skippers

Working with skippers

Liaison between the dive marshal and the skipper is vital for a good plan to evolve and an enjoyable experience to be had. Flexibility, on both sides, in response to changing conditions is key to the success of such an expedition. Good dive sites tend to be in areas with strong tides, or in restricted waters near rocks, shoal or the shore. Wrecks may reach up uncomfortably close to the surface. All of these places would normally be avoided by a vessel on a voyage.

Safety briefing

Before the start of any voyage, the skipper will brief all persons on board on the stowage and use of personal safety equipment, such as lifejackets and lifebuoys, and the procedures to be followed in an emergency.

In addition, the skipper will brief at least one other person who will be sailing on the voyage on the following points (safety cards are an acceptable way of providing this information, which is required as a part of the MCA code of practice):

- Location and launching of life rafts
- Procedure for recovering a person from the sea
- Location and use of pyrotechnics
- Operation of radios and radio procedure
- Location of navigation and other light switches
- Location and use of fire-fighting equipment
- How to stop, start and control the main engine
- How to navigate to a suitable port of refuge
- Location of the stability guidance booklet and stability information booklet if applicable.

The skipper's briefing will also include the rules of operation of the boat. There will be designated wet and dry areas on board, and possibly no-go areas. You may be asked to keep out of the wheelhouse during the process of locating the dive site, in order that the skipper can concentrate on the matter in hand.

The methods of entry into the water and recovery back onto the boat will also be explained. The skipper may request use of specific surface markers by divers and, on busy sites, they may request an additional signal from divers on the surface to identify them as belonging to their boat for pick up purposes.

The diving will be organised by the group's appointed dive marshal and an assistant dive marshal should be appointed to cover the period when the dive marshal is underwater. On a liveaboard the dive marshal is likely to be a local dive guide. The dive marshal will give a dive briefing closer to the dive time. It will include the site details such as expected depth, visibility and currents as well as any features of interest. Safety details such as the order of diving, buddy pairings, maximum dive times, divers' recall systems and procedures to be followed in the event of separation of pairs will also be discussed.

Kitting up

It is difficult to kit up if a boat is pitching heavily. To avoid this, the skipper will choose a temporary heading to reduce the motion, or seek shelter before reaching the dive site. It will help if divers can have their kit to hand, without it cluttering up deck space. If dive cylinders are being stored upright in racks, it may be possible to kit the cylinder up and place it back in the rack. Basic kit should be stored in bags or boxes until it is needed, preferably keeping buddy pairs' kit together.

Being dropped off and picked up

You should expect to enter the water at the dive site, directly from the hard boat. For particularly difficult sites, divers can be transferred to a tender for dropping off. Direct recovery of the divers by the hard boat is the normal practice of day boats in UK waters, but care must be taken if the weather is even slightly rough. Divers can also be recovered into a tender, but in any kind of sea it may be difficult to transfer divers back to the charter vessel and there will be considerable difficulty transferring equipment.

Entering the water directly from the hard boat

- Divers to be fully kitted and ready for entry
- Skipper positions the boat at the entry point
- Skipper will put the engine into neutral and inform the dive marshal
- On the dive marshal's command, divers should exit through gap or door in the gunwale, in rapid succession
- As they hit the water, divers should swim away from the boat
- Divers should signal to the dive marshal before descending

Being picked up by a hard boat

- Divers signal to the boat as soon as they surface
- Boat approaches cautiously but quickly
- Boat manoeuvres to keep divers in the lee of the vessel
- Engine is put into neutral
- Divers climb the ladder at their own pace, with help if required, or get onto a lift platform
- Crew members should be ready to receive gear and steady divers as they board

Divers signal to the dive marshal before descending

A rear-mounted lift

Remember, that compared with the strengths of boats, waves and tidal streams, divers are weak when they are in the water. You are at the mercy of wind and tide and may not even be able to catch a boat that is drifting away on a gentle wind. Consequently, when you surface in such conditions, you need to be picked up quickly. As soon as you surface, signal to the boat and prepare to be picked up.

You can expect a specially constructed diving ladder or lift to recover you onto a charter boat. A ladder should be offset from the side of the vessel, to make it easy to climb. Divers are often cold and tired at the end of a dive and a decent ladder is a welcome aid. The best type consists of a central spine with rungs projecting from each side. If this is held out from the side of the boat at an appropriate

angle a fully kitted-up diver will have no trouble getting aboard. All diving ladders should extend at least one metre below the surface in order for the diver to get a good footing. In rough seas, the pitching of the vessel will make the recovery process difficult and dangerous.

Using tenders

Rolling back to enter the water from a tender

The tender can be used to recover divers

Using tenders

An inflatable or RIB makes an ideal tender for a diving charter boat. A tender will carry the usual safety equipment, even though it may always remain close to the parent vessel. A hand-held VHF radio is ideal to make communication between the skipper and the coxswain of the tender easier. The tender is launched and recovered in the lee of the parent, usually using a boom and winch of some kind, and can be stored on davits or on deck.

Diving emergencies on charter boats

The dive marshal should be prepared for a diving emergency. You will need to know where the first-aid kit and oxygen kit are kept. It is also worth discussing with the skipper the best procedure for recovering an unconscious casualty.

Throughout any emergency, the dive marshal's role will be to liaise between the skipper and the divers and to provide the diving first aid. The skipper will liaise with the rescue services.

Entering the water from a tender

* Divers are fully kitted up, except for their fins and masks
* Divers descend the ladder into the tender
* Tender goes to the entry point
* Divers put on their fins and masks and enter the water as usual from a small boat

Recovering divers by tender

* Tender collects divers quickly and efficiently after they surface
* Divers should remove weightbelts and cylinders and stow these
* Tender comes to the lee side of the parent vessel
* Parent vessel will be stopped and in neutral
* Two divers, fore and aft of the ladder, hold the grabline of the parent vessel and steady the tender
* Other divers pass equipment up into the parent vessel, using safety lines if it is rough, before all divers climb the diving ladder

A converted fishing vessel

A purpose-built diving charter vessel

Using charter boats **167**

Appendix

Relevant extracts from the International Regulations for Preventing Collisions at Sea 1972

With amendments adopted from November 1995

Part A General

Rule 1 Application
(a)   These rules shall apply to all vessels upon the high seas and in all waters connected therewith navigable by seagoing vessels.

(b)   Nothing in these rules shall interfere with the operation of special rules made by an appropriate authority for roadsteads, harbours, rivers, lakes or inland waterways connected with the high seas and navigable by seagoing vessels. Such special rules shall conform as closely as possible to these rules.

(c)   Nothing in these rules shall interfere with the operation of any special rules made by the Government of any State with respect to additional station or signal lights, shapes or whistle signals for ships of war and vessels proceeding under convoy, or with respect to additional station or signal lights or shapes for fishing vessels engaged in fishing as a fleet. These additional station or signal lights, shapes or whistles shall, so far as possible, be such that they cannot be mistaken for any light, shape or signal authorised elsewhere under these rules.

(d)   Traffic separation schemes may be adopted by the Organisation for the purpose of these rules.

(e)   Whenever the Government concerned shall have determined that a vessel of special construction or purpose cannot comply fully with the provision of any of these rules with respect to the number, position, range or arc of visibility of lights or shapes, as well as to the disposition and characteristics of sound-signalling appliances, without interfering with the special function of the vessel, such vessel shall comply with such other provisions in regard to the number, position, range or arc of visibility of lights or shapes, as well as to the disposition and characteristics of sound-signalling appliances, as her Government shall have determined to be the closest possible compliance with these rules in respect to that vessel.

Rule 2 Responsibility
(a)   Nothing in these rules shall exonerate any vessel, or the owner, master or crew thereof, from the consequences of any neglect to comply with these rules or of the neglect of any precautions which may be required by the ordinary practice of seamen, or by the special circumstances of the case.

(b)   In construing and complying with these rules due regard shall be had to all dangers of navigation and collision and to any special circumstances, including the limitations of the vessels involved, which may make a departure from these rules necessary to avoid immediate danger.

Rule 3 General definitions
(a)   The word 'vessel' includes every description of watercraft, including non-displacement craft and seaplanes, used or capable of being used as a means of transportation on water.

(b)   The term 'power-driven vessel' means any vessel propelled by machinery.

(c)   The term 'sailing vessel' means any vessel under sail provided that propelling machinery if fitted, is not being used.

(d)   The term 'vessel engaged in fishing' means any vessel fishing with nets, lines, trawls or other fishing apparatus which restricts manoeuvrability, but does not include a vessel fishing with trolling lines or other fishing apparatus which do not restrict manoeuvrability.

(f)   The term 'vessel not under command' means a vessel which through some exceptional circumstance is unable to manoeuvre as required by these rules and is therefore unable to keep out of the way of another vessel.

(g)   The term 'vessel restricted in her ability to manoeuvre' means a vessel which from the nature of her work is restricted in her ability to manoeuvre as required by these rules and is therefore unable to keep out of the way of another vessel.

The term 'vessels restricted in their ability to manoeuvre' shall include but not be limited to:

(i)   a vessel engaged in laying, servicing or picking up a navigation mark, submarine cable or pipeline

(ii) a vessel engaged in dredging, surveying or underwater operations

(iii) a vessel engaged in replenishment or transferring persons, provisions or cargo while underway

(iv) a vessel engaged in launching or recovery of aircraft

(v)   a vessel engaged in mine clearance operations

(vi) a vessel engaged in a towing operation such as severely restricts the towing vessel and her tow in their ability to deviate from their course.

(h)   The term 'vessel constrained by her draught' means a power-driven vessel which because of her draught in relation to the available depth of water is severely restricted in her ability to deviate from the course she is following.

(i)   The word 'underway' means that a vessel is not at anchor, or made fast to the shore, or aground.

(j)   The words 'length' and 'breadth' of a vessel mean her length overall and greatest breadth.

(k)   Vessel shall be deemed to be in sight of one another only when one can be observed visually from the other.

(l)   The term 'restricted visibility' means any condition in which visibility is restricted by fog, mist, falling snow, heavy rainstorms, sandstorms or any other similar causes.

Part B Steering and sailing rules
Section 1
Conduct of vessels in any condition of visibility

Rule 5 Lookout
Every vessel shall at all times maintain a proper look-out by sight and hearing as well as by all available means appropriate in the prevailing circumstances and conditions so as to make a full appraisal of the situation and or the risk of collision.

Rule 6 Safe speed

Every vessel shall at all times proceed at a safe speed so that she can take proper and effective action to avoid a collision and be stopped within a distance appropriate to the prevailing circumstances and conditions.

In determining a safe speed the following factors shall be among those taken into account

(a) By all vessels

(i) the state of visibility

(ii) the traffic density including concentrations of fishing vessels or any other vessels

(iii) the manoeuvrability of the vessel with special reference to stopping distance and turning ability in the prevailing conditions

(iv) at night the presence of background light such as from shore lights or from back scatter of her own lights

(v) the state of wind, sea and current, and the proximity of navigational hazards

(vi) the draught in relation to the available depth of water.

(b) Additionally, by vessels with operational radar

(i) the characteristics, efficiency and limitations of the radar equipment

(ii) any constraints imposed by the radar range scale in use

(iii) the effect on radar detection of the sea state, weather and other sources of interference

(iv) the possibility that small vessels, ice and other large floating objects may not be detected by radar at an adequate range

(v) the number, location and movements of vessels detected by radar

(vi) the more exact assessment of the visibility that may be possible when radar is used to determine the range of vessels or other objects in the vicinity.

Rule 7 Risk of collision

(a) Every vessel shall use all available means appropriate to the prevailing circumstances and conditions to determine if risk of collision exists. If there is any doubt such risk shall be deemed to exist.

(b) Proper use shall be made of radar equipment if fitted and operational, including long-range scanning to obtain early warning of risk of collision and radar plotting or equivalent systematic observations of detected objects.

(c) Assumptions shall not be made on the basis of scanty information, especially scanty radar information.

(d) In determining if risk of collision exists the following considerations shall be among those taken into account

(i) such risk shall be deemed to exist if the compass bearing of an approaching vessel does not appreciably change

(ii) such risk may sometimes exist even when an appreciable bearing change is evident, particularly when approaching a very large vessel or a tow or when approaching a vessel at close range.

Rule 8 Action to avoid a collision

(a) Any action taken to avoid a collision shall, if the circumstances of the case admit, be positive, made in ample time and with due regard to the observance of good seamanship.

(b) Any alteration of course and/or speed to avoid collision shall, if the circumstances of the case admit, be large enough to be readily apparent to another vessel observing visually or by radar; a succession of small alterations of course and/or speed should be avoided.

(c) If there is sufficient sea room, alteration of course alone may be the most effective action to avoid a close-quarters situation provided that it is made in good time, is substantial and does not result in another close-quarters situation.

(d) Action taken to avoid a collision with another vessel shall be such as to result in passing at a safe distance. The effectiveness of the action shall be carefully checked until the other vessel is finally past and clear.

(e) If necessary to avoid collision or allow more time to assess the situation, a vessel shall slacken her speed or take all way off by stopping or reversing her means of propulsion.

Rule 9 Narrow channels

(a) A vessel proceeding along the course of a narrow channel or fairway shall keep as near to the outer limit or the channel or fairway which lies on her starboard side as is safe and practicable.

(b) A vessel of less than 20 metres in length or a sailing vessel shall not impede the passage of a vessel which can safely navigate only within a narrow channel or fairway.

(c) A vessel engaged in fishing shall not impede the passage of any other vessel navigating within a narrow channel or fairway.

(d) A vessel shall not cross a narrow channel of fairway if such crossing impedes the passage of a vessel which can safely navigate only within such channel or fairway. The latter vessel may use the sound signal prescribed in Rule 34 (d) if in doubt as to the intention of the crossing vessel.

(e) (i) in a narrow channel or fairway when overtaking can only take place if the vessel to be overtaken has to take action to permit safe passing, the vessel intending to overtake shall indicate her intention by sounding the appropriate signal prescribed in Rule 34 (c) (i). The vessel to be overtaken shall, if in agreement, sound the appropriate signal prescribed by Rule 34 (c) (ii) and take steps to permit safe passing. If in doubt she may sound the signals prescribed in Rule 34 (d).

(ii) this rule does not relieve the overtaking boat of her obligation under Rule 13.

(f) A vessel nearing a bend or an area of narrow channel or fairway where other vessels may be obscured by an intervening obstruction shall navigate with particular alertness and caution and shall sound the appropriate signal prescribed in Rule 34 (e).

(g) Any vessel shall, if the circumstances of the case admit, avoid anchoring in a narrow channel.

Rule 10 Traffic separation schemes

(c) A vessel shall so far as practicable avoid crossing traffic lanes, but if obliged to do so shall cross as nearly as practicable at right angles to the general direction of traffic flow.

(d) (i) inshore traffic zones shall not normally be used by through traffic which can safely use the appropriate traffic lane within the adjacent traffic separation scheme. However, vessels of less than 20 metres in length, sailing vessels and vessels engaged in fishing may under all circumstances use inshore traffic zones

(f) A vessel navigating in areas near the terminations of traffic separation schemes shall do so with particular caution.

(g) A vessel shall as far as practicable avoid anchoring in a traffic separation scheme or in areas near its terminations.

(h) A vessel not using a traffic separation scheme shall avoid it by as wide a margin as practicable.

(j) A vessel of less than 20 metres in length or a sailing vessel shall not impede the safe passage of a power-driven vessel following a traffic lane.

Section II
Conduct of vessels in sight of one another
Rule 11   Application
Rules in this section shall apply to vessels in sight of one another.

Rule 12   Sailing vessels
(a) When two sailing vessels are approaching one another, so as to involve risk of collision, one of them shall keep out of the way of the other as follows

(i) when each has the wind on a different side, the vessel which has the wind on the port side shall keep out of the way of the other

(ii) when both have the wind on the same side, the vessel which is to windward shall keep out of the way of the vessel which is to leeward

(iii) if a vessel with the wind on the port side sees a vessel to windward and cannot determine with certainty whether the other vessel has the wind on her port or starboard side, she shall keep out of the way of the other.

(b) For the purposes of this rule the windward side shall be deemed to be the side opposite to that on which the mainsail is carried or, in the case of a square-rigged vessel, the side opposite to that on which the largest fore-and-aft sail is carried.

Rule 13   Overtaking
(a) Notwithstanding anything contained in the Rules of Part B, Sections I and II, any vessel overtaking any other shall keep out of the way of the vessel being overtaken.

(b) A vessel shall be deemed to be overtaking when coming up with another vessel from a direction more than 22.5 degrees abaft her beam, that is, in such a position with reference to the vessel she is overtaking, that at night she would be able to see only the sternlight of that vessel but neither of her sidelights.

Rule 14   Head-on situation
(a) When two power-driven vessels are meeting on reciprocal or nearly reciprocal courses so as to involve risk of collision each shall alter her course to starboard so each shall pass on the port

side of the other.

Rule 15   Crossing situations
When two power-driven vessel are crossing so as to involve risk of collision, the vessel which has the other on her starboard side shall keep out of the way and shall, if the circumstances of the case admit, avoid crossing ahead of the other vessel.

Rule 18   Responsibilities between vessels
Except where rules 9, 10, and 13 otherwise require

(a) A power-driven vessel underway shall keep out of the way of

(i) a vessel not under command

(ii) a vessel restricted in ability to manoeuvre

(iii) a vessel engaged in fishing

(iv) a sailing vessel.

(b) A sailing vessel underway shall keep out of the way of

(i) a vessel not under command

(ii) a vessel restricted in ability to manoeuvre

(iii) a vessel engaged in fishing.

(c) A vessel engaged in fishing when underway shall, so far as possible, keep out of the way of

(i) a vessel not under command.

(ii) a vessel restricted in her ability to manoeuvre.

(d) (i) any vessel other than a vessel not under command or a vessel restricted in her ability to manoeuvre shall, if the circumstances of the case admit, avoid impeding the safe passage of a vessel constrained by her draught, exhibiting the signals in Rule 28.

(ii) a vessel constrained by her draught shall navigate with particular caution having full regard to her special condition.

Section III
Conduct of vessels in restricted visibility
Rule 19   Conduct of vessels in restricted visibility
(a) This rule applies to vessels not in sight of one another when navigating in or near an area of restricted visibility.

(b) Every vessel shall proceed at a safe speed adapted to the prevailing circumstances and conditions of restricted visibility. A power-driven vessel shall have her engines ready for immediate manoeuvre.

(e) Except where it has been determined that a risk of collision does not exist, every vessel which hears apparently forwards of her beam the fog signal of another vessel, or which cannot avoid a close-quarters situation with another vessel forwards of her beam, shall reduce her speed to the minimum at which she can be kept on her course. She shall if necessary take all her way off and in any event navigate with extreme caution until danger of collision is over.

Part C Lights and shapes
Rule 20   Application
(a) Rules in this Part shall be complied with in all weathers.

(b) The rules concerning lights shall be complied with from

sunset to sunrise, and during such times no other lights shall be exhibited, except such lights as cannot be mistaken for the lights specified in these Rules or do not impair their visibility or distinctive character, or interfere with the keeping of a proper look-out.

(c) The lights prescribed in these Rules shall, if carried, also be exhibited from sunrise to sunset in restricted visibility and may be exhibited in all other circumstances when it is deemed necessary.

(d) The Rules concerning shapes shall be complied with by day.

(e) The lights and shapes specified in these Rules shall comply with the provisions of Annex 1 to these Regulations.

Rule 21   Definitions
(a) "Masthead light" means a white light placed over the fore and aft centre line of the vessel showing an unbroken light over an arc of the horizon of 225 degrees and so fixed as to show the light from right ahead to 22.5 degrees abaft the beam on either side of the vessel.

(b) "Sidelights" means a green light on the starboard side and a red light on the port side each showing an unbroken light over an arc of the horizon of 112.5 degree and so fixed as to show the light from right ahead to 22.5 degrees abaft the beam on its respective side. In a vessel of less than 20 metres in length the sidelights may be combined in one lantern carried on the fore and aft centreline of the vessel.

(c) "Sternlight" means a white light placed as nearly as practicable at the stern showing an unbroken light over an arc of the horizon of 135 degrees and so fixed as to show the light 67.5 degrees from right aft on each side of the vessel.

(d) "Towing light" means a yellow light having the same characteristics as the "sternlight" defined in paragraph (c) of this Rule.

(e) "All round light" means a light showing an unbroken light over an arc of the horizon of 360 degrees.

(f) "Flashing light" means a light flashing at regular intervals at a frequency of 120 flashes or more per minute.

Rule 22   Visibility of lights
The lights prescribed in these Rules shall have an intensity as specified in Section 8 of Annex I to these Regulations so as to be visible at the following minimum ranges.

(a) In vessels of 50 metres or more in length

a masthead light, 6 miles

a sidelight, 3 miles

a sternlight, 3 miles

a towing light, 3 miles

a white, red, green or yellow all-round light, 3 miles

(b) In vessels of 12 metres or more in length but less than 50 metres in length

a masthead light, 5 miles, except where the length of the vessel is less than 20 metres, 3 miles

a sidelight, 2 miles

a sternlight, 2 miles

a towing light, 2 miles

a white, red, green or yellow all-round light, 2 miles

(c) In vessels of less than 12 metres in length

a masthead light, 2 miles

a sidelight, 1 miles

a sternlight, 2 miles

a towing light, 2 miles

a white, red, green or yellow all-round light, 2 miles

(d) In inconspicuous, partly submerged vessels or objects being towed

a masthead light, 3 miles

Rule 23   Power-driven vessels underway
(a) A power-driven vessel underway shall exhibit

(i) a masthead light forward

(ii) a second masthead light abaft and higher than the forward one; except that a vessel of less than 50m in length shall not be obliged to exhibit such light but may do so

(iii) sidelights

(iv) a sternlight.

(b) An air-cushion vessel operating in the non-displacement mode shall, in addition to the lights prescribed in paragraph (a) of this Rule, exhibit an all-round flashing yellow light.

(c) (i) a power-driven vessel of less that 12 metres in length may in lieu of the lights prescribed in paragraph (a) of this Rule exhibit an all-round white light and sidelights

(ii) a power-driven vessel of less than 7 metres in length whose maximum speed does not exceed 7 knots may in lieu of the lights prescribed in paragraph (a) of this Rule exhibit an all-round white light and shall, if practicable, also exhibit sidelights

(iii) the masthead light or all-round white light on a power-driven vessel of less than 12 metres in length may be displaced from the fore and aft centreline of the vessel if centreline fitting is not practicable, provided that the sidelights are combined in one lantern which shall be carried on the fore and aft centreline of the vessel or located as nearly as practicable in the same fore and aft line as the masthead light or the all-round white light.

Rule 26   Fishing vessels
(b) A vessel when engaged in trawling, by which is meant the dragging through the water of a dredge net of other apparatus used as a fishing appliance, shall exhibit

(i) two all-round lights in a vertical line, the upper being green and the lower white, or a shape consisting of two cones with their apexes together in a vertical line one above the other

(c) A vessel engaged in fishing, other than trawling, shall exhibit

(i) two all-round lights in a vertical line, the upper being red and the lower white, or a shape consisting of two cones with their apexes together in a vertical line one above the other; a vessel of less than 20 metres in length may instead of this shape exhibit a basket

Rule 27   Vessels not under command, or restricted in their ability to manoeuvre

(a) A vessel not under command shall exhibit

(i) two all-round red lights in a vertical line where they can best be seen

(ii) two balls or similar shapes in a vertical line where they can best be seen

(e) Whenever the size of a vessel engaged in diving operations makes it impracticable to exhibit all the lights and shapes prescribed in the paragraph (d) of this Rule, the following shall be exhibited

(i) three all-round lights in a vertical line where they can best be seen. The highest and lowest of these lights shall be red and the middle light shall be white

(ii) a rigid replica of the International Code Flag "A" not less than 1 metre in height. Measures shall be taken to ensure its all-round visibility.

(g) Vessels of less than 12 metres in length, except those engaged in diving operations shall not be required to exhibit the lights and shapes prescribed in this Rule.

Rule 28   Vessels constrained by their draught

A vessel constrained by her draught may, in addition to the lights prescribed for power-driven vessels in Rule 23, exhibit where they can best be seen three all-round red lights in a vertical line, or a cylinder.

Rule 30   Anchored vessels and vessels aground

(a) A vessel at anchor shall exhibit where it can best be seen

(i) in the fore part, an all-round white light or one ball

(ii) At or near the stern and at a lower level that the light prescribed in paragraph (I), an all-round white light.

(b) A vessel of less than 50 metres in length may exhibit an all-round white light where it can best be seen instead of the lights prescribed in paragraph (a) of this Rule.

(e) A vessel of less than 7 metres in length, when at anchor, not in or near a narrow channel, fairway or anchorage, or where other vessels normally navigate, shall not be required to exhibit the lights or shape prescribed in paragraphs (a) and (b) of this Rule.

Part D   Sound and light signals

Rule 32   Definitions

(a) The word "whistle" means any sound signalling appliance capable of producing the prescribed blasts and which complies with the specifications in Annex I of these Regulations.

(b) The term "short blast" means a blast of about one second duration.

(c) The term "prolonged blast" means a blast of about four to six seconds duration.

Rule 33   Equipment for sound signals

(a) A vessel of 12 metres or more in length shall be provided with a whistle, a vessel of 20 metres or more in length shall be provided with a bell in addition to a whistle, and a vessel of 100 metres or more in length shall, in addition, be provided with a gong, the tone and sound of which cannot be confused with that of the bell. The whistle, bell and gong shall comply with the specifications in Annex III to these Regulations.

(b) A vessel of less than 12 metres in length shall not be obliged to carry the sound signalling appliances prescribed in paragraph (a) of this Rule but if she does not, she shall be provided with some other means of making an efficient sound signal.

Rule 34   Manoeuvring and warning signals

(a) When vessel are in sight of one another, a power-driven vessel underway, when manoeuvring as authorised by these Rules, shall indicate that manoeuvre by the following signals on her whistle

- one short blast to mean "I am altering my course to starboard"
- two short blasts to mean "I am altering my course to port"
- three short blasts to mean "I am operating astern propulsion"

(b) Any vessel may supplement the whistle signals prescribed in paragraph (a) of this Rule by light signals, repeated as appropriate, whilst the manoeuvre is being carried out

(i) these signals shall have the following significance

- one flash to mean "I am altering my course to starboard"
- two flashes to mean "I am altering my course to port"
- three flashes to mean "I am operating astern propulsion"

(ii) the duration of each flash shall be about one second, the interval between flashes shall be about one second, and the interval between successive signals shall be not less that ten seconds

(iii) the light used for this signal shall, if fitted, be an all-round white light, visible at a minimum range of 5 miles, and shall comply with the provisions of Annex I of these Regulations.

(c) When in sight of one another in a narrow channel or fairway

(i) a vessel intending to overtake another shall in compliance with Rule 9 (e) (i) indicate her intention by the following signals on her whistle

- two prolonged blasts followed by one short blast to mean "I intend to overtake you on your starboard side"
- two prolonged blasts followed by two short blasts to mean "I intend to overtake you on your port side"

(ii) the vessel about to be overtaken when acting in accordance with Rule 9 (e) (i) shall indicate her agreement by the following signal on her whistle

- one prolonged, one short, one prolonged and one short blast, in that order.

(d) When vessels in sight of one another are approaching each other and from any cause either vessel either vessel fails to understand the intentions or actions of the other, or is in doubt whether sufficient action is being taken by the other to avoid collision, the vessel in doubt shall immediately indicate such doubt by giving at least five short and rapid blasts on the whistle. Such signals may be supplemented by a light signal of at least five short and rapid flashes.

(e) A vessel nearing a bend or an area of the channel of fairway where other vessels may be obscured by an intervening obstruction shall sound one prolonged blast. Such signal shall be answered with a prolonged blast by any approaching vessel that may be within hearing around the bend or behind the intervening obstruction.

Rule 35   Sound signals in restricted visibility
In or near an area of restricted visibility, whether by day or night, the signals prescribed in this Rule shall be used as follows

(a) A power-driven vessel making way through the water shall sound at intervals of not more than 2 minutes one prolonged blast.

(b) A power-driven vessel underway but stopped and making no way through the water shall sound at intervals of not more that 2 minutes two prolonged blasts in succession with an interval of about 2 seconds between them.

(c) A vessel not under command, a vessel restricted in her ability to manoeuvre, a vessel constrained by her draught, a sailing vessel, a vessel engaged in fishing and a vessel engaged in towing or pushing another vessel shall, instead of the signals prescribed in paragraphs (a) or (b) of this Rule, sound at intervals of not more that 2 minutes three blasts in succession, namely one prolonged followed by two short blasts.

(g) A vessel at anchor shall at intervals of not more than one minute ring the bell rapidly for about 5 seconds. In a vessel of 100 metres of more in length the bell shall be sounded in the forepart of the vessel and immediately after the ringing of the bell the gong shall be sounded rapidly for about 5 seconds in the after part of the vessel. A vessel at anchor may in addition sound three short blasts in succession, namely one short, one prolonged and one short blast, to give warning of her position and of the possibility of collision to an approaching vessel.

(i) A vessel of less than 12 metres in length shall not be obliged to give the above-mentioned signals but, if she does not, shall make some other efficient sound signal at intervals of not more that 2 minutes.

Rule 37   Distress signals
When a vessel is in distress and requires assistance she shall use or exhibit the signals described in Annex IV to these Regulations.

Annex iv

Distress signals
1. The following signals, used or exhibited either together or separately, indicate distress and need of assistance:

(a) a gun or other explosive signal fired at intervals of about a minute;

(b) a continuous sounding with any fog-signalling apparatus;

(c) rockets or shells, throwing red stars fired one at a time at short intervals;

(d) a signal made by radiotelegraphy or by any other signalling method consisting of the group . . . - - - . . . (SOS) in the Morse Code;

(e) a signal sent by radiotelephony consisting of the spoken word 'Mayday';

(f) the International Code Signal of distress indicated by N.C;

(g) a signal consisting of a square flag having above or below it a ball or anything resembling a ball;

(h) flames on the vessel (as from a burning barrel, oil barrel, etc.);

   (i) a rocket parachute flare or hand flare showing a red light;

   (j) a smoke signal giving off orange-coloured smoke;

(k) slowly and repeatedly raising and lowering arms outstretched to each side;

(l) the radiotelegraph alarm signal;

(m) the radiotelephone alarm signal;

(n) signals transmitted by emergency position-indicating radio beacons.

(o) approved signals transmitted by radio-communication systems, including survival craft radar transponders.

2. The use or exhibition of any of the foregoing signals except for the purpose of indicating distress and need of assistance and the use of other signals, which may be confused with any of the above signals is prohibited.

3. Attention is drawn to the relevant sections of the International Code of Signals, the Merchant Ship Search and Rescue Manual and the following signals:

(a) a piece of orange-coloured canvas with either a black square and circle or other appropriate symbol (for identification from the air);

(b) a dye marker.

Index

Useful organisations

Useful organisations

British Sub-Aqua Club
www.bsac.org
Safe diving practice and many other links to useful, diving-related sites

International Maritime Organization
www.imo.org
International Rules for the Prevention of Collisions at Sea, International Convention on Safety of Life At Sea, International Convention for the Prevention of Pollution from Ships

Maritime and Coastguard Agency
www.mcga.gov.uk
All aspects of safety at sea in UK waters

The Met Office
www.met-office.gov.uk
Weather forecasting

National Trailer and Towing Association
www.ntta.co.uk
UK towing guidelines

The UK Hydrographic Office
www.ukho.gov.uk
Admiralty charts and publications, on-line tidal predictions

Acknowledgements

Lizzie Bird BSAC
Trevor Davies BSAC
Mark Allen BSAC
Clare Peddie BSAC
Jim Watson BSAC
Alistair Reynolds BSAC
Mary Tetley BSAC
Marcus Allen BSAC
RAF 722 Squadron (Chivenor)
Ken Bazeley MRCC Falmouth
Barnet Marine
Bournemouth Barracudas BSAC 2002
EXUL BSAC 320
Potters Bar BSAC 714